TEACHING AND LEARNING IN STEM WITH COMPUTATION, MODELING, AND SIMULATION PRACTICES

TEACHING AND LEARNING IN STEM WITH COMPUTATION, MODELING, AND SIMULATION PRACTICES

A Guide for Practitioners and Researchers

Alejandra J. Magana

Purdue University Press · West Lafayette, Indiana

Cataloging-in-Publication Data is on file with the Library of Congress.
978-1-61249-926-0 (print)
978-1-61249-927-7 (epub)
978-1-61249-928-4 (epdf)

Cover: Composite image using the following assets: monsitj/iStock via Getty Images;
maxkabakov/iStock via Getty Images

I dedicate this to my family,
for your constant love and support;
and to my collaborators and mentors,
for your advocacy and the
opportunity to learn from you

CONTENTS

APPENDICES   69

FOREWORD

FOR CENTURIES, WE SCIENTISTS AND ENGINEERS HAVE CREATED MATHEMATICAL models of physical objects and processes. Early astronomers predicted the future positions of the planets by modeling their motions with Kepler's laws, which specify mathematically the shape of an orbit and the variations in orbital speed. Engineers estimated fluid pressures by modeling hydraulic systems with control-volume analysis.

As our understandings of the natural and constructed worlds deepened, our mathematical models became larger and more sophisticated. To efficiently perform the calculations required by these larger models, we started using electromechanical calculators and digital computers. With computers, we can process large amounts of data to forecast the weather every day. Large datasets are used by machine learning algorithms in many contemporary applications of artificial intelligence, such as diagnostic radiology and voice recognition. The outputs of computational simulations are often visualizations of processes, such as the gradual evolution of a forest in a warming climate, and the rapid drift of electrons in a field-effect transistor. These visualizations display slow and fast processes on a human time scale.

To prepare future scientists and engineers to use computation in their professional careers, classroom instructors have begun to incorporate learning activities in which students develop computational models and perform computational simulations. To use computation successfully, students should learn more than how to enter data into a commercial software package for computational fluid dynamics. They should be prepared to think carefully as they write the code that defines a computational model. They should be able to identify the limitations and potential errors, such as ineluctable errors in converting the continuous variables of a mathematical model into the discrete variables of a computational model. The question is, How can instructors teach computational concepts and thinking skills effectively?

Recently, studies of computational thinking have been conducted by education researchers as one strand of discipline-based education research (DBER) in science and engineering. DBER publications are intended to be read by other DBER researchers, not by classroom instructors. For example, articles in the *Journal of Engineering Education*, for which I served as the editor for five years, would be difficult for engineering instructors to understand—we DBER researchers have enough difficulty understanding these articles ourselves! Thus, there is a great need to synthesize the findings of DBER studies into recommendations for classroom instructors. This synthesis effort is an important, underappreciated form of scholarship.

In this book, Alejandra Magana and her associates bring the findings of DBER studies on computational thinking to a broad audience of classroom instructors across all science and engineering subjects. The book applies state-of-the-art instructional frameworks to structure comprehensive instructional modules for computational modeling and simulation and offers examples of actual instructional modules for a high school course, for two first-year college courses, and for a capstone design course for advanced undergraduates. The modules include prompts for students to think critically as they design and debug computational models to solve authentic problems and emphasize that students should validate and verify their models.

In summary, I believe that this book will guide and inspire instructors to create learning activities that teach skills in computational modeling and simulation, essential skills that will enable students to become effective scientists and engineers in this century.

MICHAEL C. LOUI
PROFESSOR EMERITUS OF ELECTRICAL AND COMPUTER ENGINEERING
UNIVERSITY OF ILLINOIS URBANA-CHAMPAIGN

PREFACE

COMPUTING HAS BECOME THE THIRD PILLAR OF SCIENCE AND ENGINEERING, DRIV-
ing discovery and innovation in industry and academia. In addition, the modern workforce must be equipped with computing skills to fulfill the job market demands. As a
result, faculty members in higher education institutions have integrated computational
methods and tools into their teaching in the form of computation, modeling, and simulation practices. However, doing this integration successfully is not easy for faculty
members due to packed curricula, among other difficulties, nor for their students due
to the integration of multiple concepts and skills (i.e., mathematics, engineering, programming). These difficulties often result in computation, modeling, and simulation
practices largely left untaught or narrowly introduced at the undergraduate level in the
context of science and engineering courses, except those for computer science and electrical engineering majors.

One way in which faculty have identified methods to integrate computation, modeling, and simulation practices in undergraduate education is by deploying computational learning modules as project assignments (e.g., two or three small projects within
a semester-long course). Such modules have mainly been deployed as homework assignments, final projects, or term projects. However, the issue of students experiencing
learning difficulties is hard to address without implementing proper learning strategies
and pedagogical methods. That is, while learning challenges can be addressed when
the instructor or the teaching assistant is present in the classroom, students mainly engage with the computational assessments outside of the classroom (i.e., as take-home
assignments). In those instances, precisely, students need pedagogical support to guide
them in recalling prior knowledge and applying learning strategies to approach learning challenges. Supporting students' learning processes within, but more importantly
outside of, the classroom is the main motivation for this book.

This instructor's guide is addressed to faculty members in higher education institutions who want to integrate modeling and simulation practices within science, technology, engineering, and mathematics (STEM) disciplinary courses. It is also addressed to
discipline-based education researchers who engage in the scholarship of teaching and
learning with the goals of (1) improving the students' learning and expertise development and (2) contributing with new knowledge in their corresponding fields. The author assumes that the reader has the disciplinary knowledge and computational skills
to do so. Thus, this guide focuses on the instructional (how to design learning experiences), pedagogical (how to deliver and support the learning experiences), and educational research (what new knowledge can be derived from the interventions) aspects. In
addition to providing guidance on designing, delivering, and evaluating instructional

interventions in the context of computation, modeling, and simulation practices, this guide also provides a collection of exemplary computational assignments.

This work results from more than 15 years of conducting education research in and out of undergraduate STEM classroom settings. It also has had implications for K–12 education. Each classroom implementation has been performed closely between engineering or science education researchers and the course instructor who implemented a specific module or lesson. Each module or instructional unit presented in this guide has been iteratively refined based on the findings. The author and the collaborating contributors hope that the readers and their students successfully integrate computation, modeling, and simulation practices sooner, better, and with greater success.

INTRODUCTION

ADVANCEMENTS IN CYBERINFRASTRUCTURE ALLOWING THE DEPLOYMENT OF LARGE-scale simulations along with the deluge of accumulated scientific data have revolutionized scientific and engineering disciplines. Furthermore, new disciplines such as simulation-based and computational and data-enabled engineering and science, among others, have now been recognized as distinct intellectual and technological disciplines residing at the intersection of mathematics, statistics, computer science, and science and engineering disciplines. While science and engineering disciplines take advantage of these advancements by adopting new tools and practices to support discovery and innovation, science and engineering education lags behind in instilling in future graduates the ability to infer meaning from data collected from measurements or computational simulations.

To take steps toward closing this gap between research and industry needs and academic preparation for the 21st-century skills, this guide provides a practical approach, along with examples of curricular materials that can assist faculty in adopting these practices as part of their disciplinary courses. It also follows an approach to understanding by design (Wiggins and McTighe 1997, 2005), which aligns the content and practices being learned with acceptable evidence of learning, along with the planning and delivery of the experiences and instructional approach.

This instructor's guide is organized as follows. Chapter 1 motivates the work and introduces the theoretical foundation of model-based reasoning for developing understandings and skills associated with computation, modeling, and simulation practices. Chapter 2 describes our approach to understanding by design for integrating computation, modeling, and simulation practices in undergraduate STEM education. Specifically, this chapter proposes a curricular framework for introducing modeling and simulation practices throughout the undergraduate curriculum in STEM disciplines. We then propose assessment guidelines for evaluating students' performance when solving modeling and simulation challenges, followed by pedagogical strategies and methods informed by evidence-based practices.

Chapter 3 presents a selection of curricular designs that integrate computation, modeling, and simulation practices for different audiences and contexts. The audiences range from K–12 learners to novice and advanced undergraduate learners. The context and scope range from classroom activities to support disciplinary learning, to implementation in the laboratory to support experimentation, to integration in a capstone design course through an extended period of time, to being part of a K–12 science classroom.

Chapter 4 elaborates on the theoretical foundation of research pertaining to the integration of computation, modeling, and simulation in undergraduate STEM education, summarizes findings from more than a decade of research in this area, and proposes a pedagogical framework called a computational cognitive apprenticeship. This chapter also elaborates on opportunities for future research.

CHAPTER 1 MOTIVATES THE INTEGRATION OF COMPUTATION, MODELING, AND SIM-
ulation practices in STEM education and provides the theoretical foundation for developing understandings and skills associated with computation, modeling, and simulation practices. We first define models and modeling as well as a simulation in the context of STEM education. We then characterize model-based reasoning as the primary underlying thought process when engaging in modeling and simulation practices.

MODELS, MODELING, AND SIMULATION

A model is referred to as an abstract, simplified representation of a system or a phenomenon that makes its essential features explicit and visible so that it can be used to generate explanations and predictions (Harrison and Treagust 2000). Representational models, such as diagrams, graphs, simulations, or equations, are central to scientific research (Bowen, Roth, and McGinn 1999) as well as to the solution of complex problems in workplace engineering (Jonassen, Strobel, and Lee 2006). Models are used in engineering to gain insight into the material world (Carlson 2003), further interpret information about a problem (Higley et al. 2007), identify relationships between its components (Brophy and Li 2010), and provide the potential for new solutions to it (Jonassen, Strobel, and Lee 2006).

Modeling practices refer to the processes of constructing analogical models and reasoning through manipulating them. This ability develops as people learn domain-specific content and techniques (Nersessian 1999). Reasoning with models entails the formation of a conception of the mental model first, followed by further abstraction to create a formal expression in the form of a mathematical model, law, axiom, or theory (Nersessian 1999). Modeling is a powerful cognitive tool because it simplifies the complexities of the real world, allowing us to concentrate our attention on the aspects that are of greatest interest or significance (Feurzeig and Roberts 1999). Creating this formal expression involves (a) the representation of one system by another, (b) the self-conscious separation of a model and its referent, (c) the explicit consideration of measurement error, and (d) the understanding of alternative models (Lehrer and Schauble 2000).

In science and engineering practice, modeling and simulation processes are combined in an iterative cycle where a phenomenon is studied or a system under study is altered. Modeling consists of producing a model to represent the inner workings of a system. Simulation refers to the operation of a model that can be reconfigured and explored (Maria 1997). Specifically, scientific modeling practices identify key aspects of a theory and evidence in an expressed representation, use the representation to illustrate, predict, and explain phenomena, and evaluate and revise the representation as it is used (Schwarz et al. 2009). Engineering modeling practices require both the ability to produce, manipulate, interpret, and reinterpret models and the ability to comprehend equivalences in different modes of expression and to learn, transform, and apply information from one representation to another (Sigel 1999). A computational simulation is often used to perform mathematical experimentation to aid these processes so that individuals connect observed phenomena with their underlying models and causal processes (Feurzeig and Roberts 1999).

Closely related practices to modeling and simulation are computation practices. Computation practices refer to the use of advanced computing capabilities to understand and solve complex problems by developing and using mathematical models. In the context of science and engineering, different classes of mathematical equations need to be constantly related to the modeling of physical systems (Bellomo and Preziosi 1994). Some of the mathematical models can be solved by analytic methods, but others require numerical techniques. Thus, computation is necessary to approach the solution of problems relating to the analysis of models (Bellomo and Preziosi 1994). Problems requiring numerical techniques are often nonlinear, making them solvable only by computational methods. Thus, engaging with models—conceptual, mathematical, and computational—is at the core of computation, modeling, and simulation practices.

MODEL-BASED REASONING AND IMPLICATIONS FOR EDUCATION

The ability to create models or representations from existing ones has been referred to as model-based reasoning (Nersessian 2002). That is, model-based reasoning entails abstracting physical phenomena into some form of a representational model. These models are either created or adapted, connecting or transforming them into other representational forms such as equations or computational models during problem-solving episodes (Nersessian 2002).

Previous research has identified the reasoning processes associated with modeling activities, including the following (Löhner et al. 2005; Shiflet and Shiflet 2014):

Analyzing the problem, where the objective is determined, and the type of problem is identified.

Formulating the problem, where the problem is decomposed and then articulated into a model. During problem formulation sub-steps are also determined, such as gathering data, making assumptions and simplifications, determining variables and relationships between variables, and determining equations and functions.

Implementing the model, which involves using different methods, techniques, and computational tools at the same time as making assumptions and simplifications as they build or configure the model.

Solving the model, which consists of executing the model multiple times, interpreting the output of the model, and synthesizing the results and findings.

Verifying and validating the model, which consist of determining whether the solution works correctly and the model satisfies the problem's requirements.

Reporting the model, which concerns the documenting of the model design and model solution, reporting results and conclusions, and recording assumptions and limitations.

Maintaining the model, which consists of making desirable improvements, corrections, and enhancements.

When promoted in educational settings, these reasoning processes have been referred to as model-based learning and teaching. Model-based learning refers to the knowledge and skills gained from constructing models, using and evaluating models, and revising and elaborating models (Gobert and Buckley 2000; Louca and Zacharia 2012; Schwarz et al. 2009). Model-based teaching refers to the instructional conditions that implement learning activities intended to facilitate model-building at the individual and group levels. These learning activities must be orchestrated and sequenced following a proper pedagogy and also well supported with scaffolding (Gobert and Buckley 2000). Scaffolding refers to all types of support and guidance offered in and outside of the classroom either by the instructor, peers, or technology (Boblett 2012). The chapters that follow provide design principles and samples of learning activities that bring together model-based teaching and learning to engage learners in modeling and simulation practices.

2

CHAPTER 2 PRESENTS A FRAMEWORK THAT ALIGNS THE ESSENTIAL ELEMENTS FOR designing and implementing computation, modeling, and simulation practices into STEM disciplinary coursework. Essential elements required for an instructional design and implementation can be described through understanding by design (Wiggins and McTighe 1997, 2005). Understanding by design is a model or framework that emphasizes a set of tools and practices that consist of three stages: (1) identifying the desired learning outcomes (the content and practices to be learned), (2) determining the acceptable evidence of learning (the method of assessing learning), and (3) planning the experiences and instructional approach (or pedagogy).

Based on the understanding by design framework, we first propose a curricular framework for introducing computation, modeling, and simulation practices throughout the undergraduate curriculum in STEM disciplines. We then propose assessment guidelines for evaluating students' performance when solving computation, modeling, and simulation challenges. Finally, we also propose pedagogical strategies and scaffolding methods informed by the cognitive apprenticeship model. Cognitive apprenticeship is a model of instruction that deliberately addresses the reasoning processes associated with performing a task or solving a problem, making them visible or explicit to the learner (Collins, Brown, and Newman 1989).

A CURRICULAR FRAMEWORK FOR INTEGRATING MODELING AND SIMULATION PRACTICES

An important step when designing learning experiences is to clearly specify what students must learn and do to complete a lesson or course. However, decisions about learning outcomes need to be taken within some specific context and with a particular audience in mind. Context and audience definitions allow instructors to make explicit assumptions about previous knowledge. This precise initial approach is also needed when integrating computation, modeling, and simulation practices into our curriculum.

In our previous work (Magana and Coutinho 2017), we distinguished different computing audiences by following Hu's (2007) work. In that study, Hu made a distinction between computation skills for "the specialists" and computation skills for "the crowds." Hu (2007) identified the crowds as engineers, scientists, and mathematicians evaluating and using computation and the specialists as computational scientists, engineers,

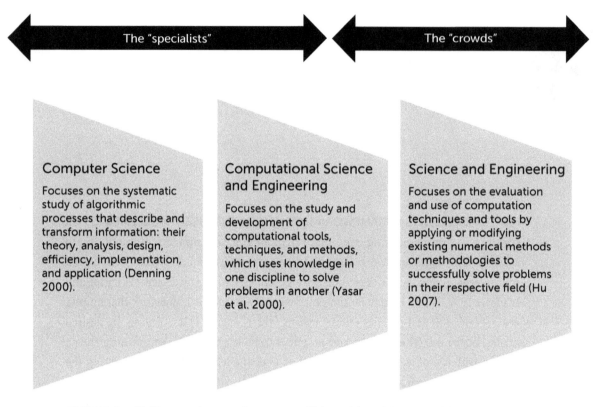

FIGURE 2.1 Different audiences of computing. (Adapted from Magana and Coutinho 2017.)

and mathematicians who, in addition, create computational tools and algorithms. As shown in figure 2.1, we proposed that a crowds approach is needed for integrating computation, modeling, and simulation practices for STEM domains. We argued that students in STEM majors need to become proficient at integrating computation, modeling, and simulation for the crowds. As proposed in figure 2.1, in a crowds perspective, as opposed to a specialist perspective, students in STEM domains need to develop the knowledge and skills that enable them to identify when, why, and how computation methods work and don't work. They must also be able to apply or modify existing numerical methods or methodologies to successfully solve problems or design solutions (Hu 2007). Excellent learning materials and resources have been created for the specialists, such as the book *Introduction to Computational Science: Modeling and Simulation for the Sciences* by Angela Shiflet and George Shiflet (2014). In comparison, our book focuses on supports for teaching and learning computation, modeling, and simulation practices for the crowds.

Once the context and target audience have been identified, we can define the learning objectives. Disciplinary faculty often focus their learning objectives on the subject domain, but specific practices are sometimes assumed. We would like to emphasize that in addition to identifying specific learning objectives within specific disciplinary courses, it is also important to thoughtfully identify computation, modeling, and simulation practices and corresponding objectives in parallel.

In our previous work, we proposed a learning progression. A learning progression refers to a purposeful sequencing of teaching and learning expectations across multiple grade levels for using, creating, evaluating, and revising models suitable for the crowds (Magana 2017). These expectations can directly inform the identification of learning objectives related to computational, modeling, and simulation practices. This learning progression can be used as a guideline for integrating modeling and simulation practices within disciplinary courses in STEM. Specifically, our learning progression represents a logical roadmap that can guide the coherent development of curriculum, assessment, and instruction (Corcoran, Mosher, and Rogat 2009). The learning progression was derived from eight national reports from organizations such as the US Department of Defense (two reports), the US Department of Energy (one report), the US National Science Foundation (three reports), the Association of Computing Machinery and IEEE (one report), and an introductory book to modeling and simulation for the sciences (Magana and Coutinho 2017). The learning progression was later revised and validated by 37 science and engineering experts from industry and academia as part of a three-round Delphi study (Magana 2017).

The proposed learning progression is organized into three levels of achievement, each organized in practices consisting of constructing, using, evaluating, and revising models. The levels indicate higher-order learning goals. In the following sections, we present each level and the corresponding practices.

Level 1: Essential Modeling and Simulation Skills

Level 1 is characterized by practices that can be integrated into the first and second years of undergraduate education. These practices are also the ones identified as essential for STEM graduates. Table 2.1 describes the practices and performances for Level 1.

TABLE 2.1 *Practices and performances for Level 1*

Practice	Performance
Constructing models	Students construct visual representations of data, such as graphs, charts, tables, and histograms, using standard domain-specific software, application programming interfaces, or built-in libraries within scientific computing software. Given a simple model, students identify the corresponding mathematical model and use computer programming methods or APIs to implement an appropriate algorithm representing abstractions of reality via mathematical formulas, constructions, equations, inequalities, constraints, and so forth.
Using models	Students use existing computational models or simulations to comprehend, characterize, and draw conclusions from visual representations of data by evaluating appropriate boundary conditions, noticing patterns, identifying relationships, assessing situations, and so forth.
Evaluating models	Students compare the results of models and simulations to laboratory experiments, theory, measurements, test cases, and so forth to determine their alignment, overlap, or goodness of fit, among other metrics.
Revising models	Students extend or adapt simple models from one situation to another, either by configuring the model through a graphical user interface or by modifying or extending existing code.

TABLE 2.2 *Practices and performances for Level 2*

Practice	Performance
Constructing models	Students connect simulation and visualization by first visualizing data using numerical outputs from a simulation and then interacting with the visualization to engage in critical thinking about the simulated model. Students implement simple computational models by creating discretized mathematical descriptions of an event or phenomenon using high-level programming languages or scientific computing software.
Using models	Students use simulations at different scales to deploy the correct solution method, inputs, and other parameters to explore theories and identify relationships between modeled phenomena. Students use computational models or simulations to design, modify, or optimize materials, processes, products, or systems. Students use computational models or simulations to design experiments to test theories, prototypes, products, materials, and so forth. Students use computational models or simulations to infer and predict physical phenomena or the behaviors of engineered systems.
Evaluating models	Students evaluate the benefits and disadvantages of competing computational models or simulations by determining and weighing factors such as assumptions, limitations, precision, accuracy, reliability, validity, and complexity. Students acknowledge and estimate uncertainty as part of the interpretation of simulation predictions.
Revising models	Students use external data, theories, or additional simulation tools to calibrate, verify, or improve the accuracy of computational models or simulations.

Level 2: Highly Desirable Modeling and Simulation Skills

Level 2 modeling and simulation practices are characterized by those skills that can be integrated into the third and fourth years of undergraduate education. These practices are more complex than the ones presented in Level 1 and were identified as highly desired for industry and academic settings. Table 2.2 describes the practices and performances for Level 2.

Level 3: Specialized Modeling and Simulation Skills

Level 3 modeling and simulation practices are characterized by highly complex skills integrated into advanced degrees (i.e., master's and doctoral students). These skills are more specialized and often needed for research and development purposes. Table 2.3 describes the practices and performances for Level 3.

Once the learning objectives have been identified, the next step is to align the assessment with those specific learning objectives. In a way, the learning objective is already prescribing the assessment method. For example, if the learning objective is associated with modeling practices of constructing models, it is then necessary that the assessment would consist of evaluating the models students built. We elaborate more on the assessment in the following section.

TABLE 2.3 *Practices and performances for Level 3*

Practice	Performance
Constructing models	Students construct new computational models or simulations by developing algorithms and methods that simulate physical phenomena and engineered systems.
Using models	Students interface computational models or simulations directly with measurement devices such as sensors, imaging systems, real-time control systems, and so forth.
Evaluating models	Students discern between different algorithms or computational methods to describe physical models or engineered systems as computational representations. Students determine and quantify the reliability of computer simulations and their predictions. Students determine variability in data due to immeasurable or unknown factors via uncertainty quantification methods or techniques. Students evaluate algorithms by determining uncertainties and defining error, stability, machine precision concepts, and the inexactness of computational approximations (e.g., convergence, including truncation and round-off). Students verify a simulation model based on software engineering protocols, bug detection and control, and scientific programming methods. Students validate a simulation model based on prescribed acceptance criteria such as observations, experiments, experience, and judgment.
Revising models	Students identify the mechanisms for exchanging information to bridge models across scales and maintain computational tractability. Students iteratively and systematically evaluate and improve their computational models or simulations' fidelity, accuracy, reliability, performance, and cost (monetary and computational).

ASSESSMENT GUIDELINES FOR MODELING AND SIMULATION PRACTICES

The attainment of modeling and simulation skills is difficult to assess. Especially in higher education, in the context of STEM courses, one form of assessment often used is examinations, which evaluate multiple learning outcomes at a time. For instance, mid-semester and final semester examinations may assess the learning of concepts, the application of a mathematical formulation to represent a problem, including accurate calculations resulting in a value, and the creation or interpretation of graphs representing cause–effect relationships, among others. However, we advocate that for assessing computation, modeling, and simulation practices, we need assessment methods for higher-order skills. In such assessments, students are elicited to demonstrate their applied knowledge, creativity, problem-solving, and critical thinking skills, where a careful alignment between intended learning outcomes and evidence of the learning is critical. A tool that permits the careful alignment between intended learning outcomes and evidence of the learning is Pellegrino's assessment triangle (Pellegrino, Chudowsky, and Glaser 2001), as shown in figure 2.2.

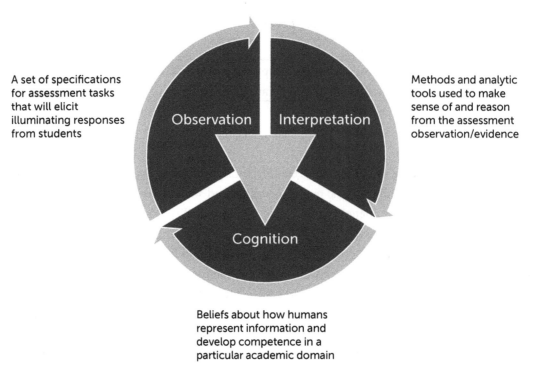

A set of specifications for assessment tasks that will elicit illuminating responses from students

Observation

Interpretation

Methods and analytic tools used to make sense of and reason from the assessment observation/evidence

Cognition

Beliefs about how humans represent information and develop competence in a particular academic domain

FIGURE 2.2 Pellegrino's assessment triangle. (Adapted from Pellegrino, Chudowsky, and Glaser 2001.)

Figure 2.2 portrays the assessment triangle (inverted) that assists educators in designing assessments focused on three key elements: (1) a model of student *cognition* based on beliefs about how individuals represent information and develop competence in a particular domain; (2) *observations* consisting of the evidence of students' competencies that take the form of tasks that elicit responses from students; and (3) *interpretations* that make sense of the evidence, usually in the form of analytic tools. Applying the guidance from Pellegrino's assessment triangle to evaluate modeling and simulation practices, we used the assessment triangle shown in figure 2.3.

Model-based reasoning refers to a form of thinking associated with how individuals make sense of or represent phenomena (including processes, systems, or products) by using or creating external representations in the form of models (Johnson-Laird 1995). As shown in figure 2.3, model-based reasoning is the main intended learning, thus representing the model of *cognition*. Based on our curricular framework for integrating modeling and simulation practices, the *observations* associated with model-based reasoning need to elicit practices such as constructing models, using models, evaluating models, and revising models (i.e., the model-eliciting activities in figure 2.3), as described in tables 2.1, 2.2, and 2.3. The overt processes students followed or the artifacts they created can represent evidence of such observations. For *interpretation* of the observations, a common practice is the use of rubrics evaluating criteria based on specified levels of performance. We now elaborate on these ideas.

VanLehn (2013) identified that the process of model construction can be assessed in terms of *product* and *process*. Product assessment focuses on evaluating the quality of artifacts (i.e., models) that students constructed, typically by identifying their level of correctness and acceptability. Also, a common assessment approach in the product

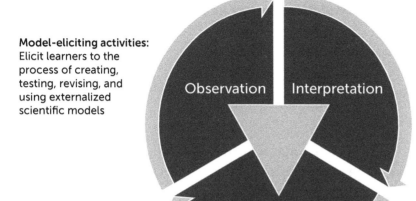

Model-eliciting activities: Elicit learners to the process of creating, testing, revising, and using externalized scientific models

Assessment rubrics: Focus on the process and the artifacts students generated; can focus on metacognitive processes too

Observation   Interpretation

Cognition

Model-based reasoning: A form of thinking associated with how individuals make sense of phenomena through different forms of external representations in the form of models

FIGURE 2.3 Application of the assessment triangle for modeling and simulation skills.

category involves identifying students' increased or enhanced existing domain knowledge. Process assessment focuses on evaluating students' behaviors when constructing models and their ability to transfer those skills for the construction of similar models. We suggest an evaluation approach that mainly focuses on products and processes directly associated with the modeling and simulation process. However, at the end of this section, we also explore other common assessment forms in this context.

To identify whether students have acquired computation, modeling, and simulation skills, it would be first necessary to identify whether they have engaged in model-based reasoning. Evidence of engagement in model-based reasoning would include behaviors associated with the modeling and simulation process. For instance, has the student analyzed the problem, decomposed it, and then articulated it into a model? Has the student identified the proper mathematical formulation and implemented a functional numerical solution in the form of a computational simulation? Has the student engaged in validation and verification processes to evaluate their solution? Has the student used the model to solve the science or engineering problem?

Here we propose that modeling and simulation skills be assessed in processes and products. Processes and products could be evaluated together by eliciting students' rationale and explanations in the form of a final report, along with the produced computational model (i.e., the actual executable file). Guidance to create a final report can be provided in the form of a template. The template ought to provide some guidance on what ideas should be described in each section of the report. Figure 2.4 presents a sample of a template.

Template for a Modeling and Simulation Project Report

1. **Describe the Problem**

   [Determine the problem's objective and identify its characteristics.]

2. **Frame the Problem**

   [Conduct a literature review to contextualize your problem and investigate the properties of your model.]

3. **Configure the Model**

   [Define a model that will help you solve the problem (define goals, information, assumptions, boundary conditions) in terms of relevant models, concepts, or theories used in class or from the literature. Identify assumptions and limitations.]

4. **Validate the Model**

   [Establish whether the simulation satisfies the problem's requirements. You can validate it by testing simple scenarios, by developing your own "toy" model (e.g., a MATLAB code of a simple test case), by means of experimental conditions under the same assumptions, using a theoretical model, or by means of test cases using another computational tool.]

5. **Verify the Model**

   [Examine the results to determine whether the solution works correctly (verification) via testing the solution to see if predictions agree with real data, data from industry standards, or data published in scientific papers.]

6. **Solve the Problem**

   [Show and explain your solution. Interpret the output and show how the proposed solution addressed the problem/project. Identify limitations along with ranges of operation. Determine whether the system works; if it does not work, provide an explanation/justification of why.]

FIGURE 2.4 Sample template for a project report. (Adapted from Shaikh et al. 2015.)

In addition to the report template and additional instructions to also submit their executable files with the implementations of their models, students should be provided with a rubric that details performance levels and criteria to be evaluated. We suggest the following six-step procedure for creating a rubric:

1. Select the desired modeling and simulation practices or performances from tables 2.1, 2.2, or 2.3, accordingly.
2. Identify how those practices and performances can be demonstrated by the students either in terms of process or outcome.
3. Transform those processes or outcomes into detailed criteria to be evaluated.
4. Determine weighting for each criterion based on the level of effort required or importance.
5. Set standards for levels of performance for each of the criteria (e.g., poor, basic, proficient, and advanced) and determine the scoring in terms of points.
6. Identify observable factors that provide the basis for assessing which level of performance has been achieved and describe those factors within each cell for student and grader reference.

Table 2.4 provides a sample rubric. This rubric can be used to evaluate students' reports as well as their created computational solutions. It was particularly designed for the practices of constructing models (criteria 1, 2, and 3 from table 2.4), evaluating models (criterion 3 from table 2.4), and using models (criterion 4 from table 2.4). Although the criteria presented in the rubric have been more generally described, they can be aligned further with specific performances from tables 2.1, 2.2, and 2.3.

Assessment methods can also evaluate the knowledge that results from engaging in modeling and simulation practices. We briefly discuss other assessment mechanisms proposed by VanLehn (2013). Assessments that evaluate learning or new knowledge that resulted from engaging in modeling and simulation practices often take the form of written exams or tests where students can be asked to do the following:

- Make predictions in the form of "what if" questions that demonstrate student understanding of cause–effect relationships.
- Sketch or interpret graphs demonstrating the relationship between two variables or the value of a variable over time.
- Construct explanations describing certain behaviors, including the evidence of such behavior.
- Solve problems based on scenarios that prompt students to identify a mathematical model to solve the problem and perform handwritten calculations to solve it.
- Demonstrate conceptual understanding by explaining a concept.

TABLE 2.4 *Sample rubric for a project report*

Criteria	Poor (0–3)	Basic (3–5)	Proficient (5–8)	Advanced (9–10)
PROBLEM DESCRIPTION (20%) Describe the problem that is proposed to be solved and provide a justification using literature from relevant research papers.	An unclear description of the problem statement and no relevant research backing provided.	Description of the problem statement needs refinement. Inadequate research relevance.	The problem is defined appropriately but needs a little more refinement in terms of relevant literature.	The problem is very well defined, and the literature from relevant research work builds a perfect case for the problem.
PROBLEM FRAMING: CONCEPTUAL (10%); MATHEMATICAL (10%) Build both a conceptual model and a mathematical model to solve the problem. Interpret the problem (goals, information, limitations, and assumptions) in terms of relevant models, concepts, or theories.	No conceptual or mathematical model is included in the report.	Both a conceptual and a mathematical model are provided but are incorrect.	Both a conceptual and a mathematical model are provided but need minor improvements.	Both the conceptual and mathematical models provided accurately frame the problem.

Continued

TABLE 2.4 *Continued*

Criteria	Poor (0–3)	Basic (3–5)	Proficient (5–8)	Advanced (9–10)
PROBLEM SYNTHESIS: BUILD (15%); VALIDATE (10%) Evaluate the quality of the solution approach built to solve the problem. The simulation or program needs to be validated thoroughly with either experimental data or test cases. Predictively compare and contrast alternate solution processes in terms of relevant metrics (e.g., accuracy, precision, efficiency, reliability, feasibility, risk, impact). Use a simulation or build your own program that will help you solve the problem.	The implementation of the solution approach is incorrect. The solution approach is not validated.	The implementation of the solution approach serves the purpose but needs to be refined. The validation process for the solution approach needs to be improved.	The implementation of the solution approach provides the approach to solve the problem but needs minor improvements. The validation process for the solution approach needs minor improvements.	The implementation of the solution approach is accurate. The solution approach is validated appropriately.
PROBLEM SOLUTION AND INTERPRETATION OF FINDINGS (30%) Determine whether the executable code (i.e., the computational model) addresses the disciplinary issue and solves a related problem. Explain the output of the model and how it solves the problem.	No solution was provided to the problem. Does not discuss the application of a solution for a related problem.	A solution is provided, but it is incorrect or does not adequately address the issue or problem. Not a clear description of how the solution can be used to resolve a related problem.	A solution is provided that would adequately address the issue or problem, but it is presented in a way that is unclear or improperly documented. A discussion is included, which describes the use of the current approach to solving related problems.	A solution is provided that is correct, clear, and well-documented. A very clear description is included, which describes the use of the current approach to solving related problems.
ORGANIZATION OF THE REPORT (5%) Provide appropriate structure, sentence construction, and grammar.	The report is not well structured and contains 10 or more grammatical or sentence construction errors.	The report contains 5 to 9 grammatical or sentence construction errors.	The report is structured well and contains less than 5 grammatical or sentence construction errors.	The report contents are well structured. The report contains no grammatical or sentence construction errors.

Source: Fennell et al. (2017).

No assessment is perfect, but by focusing on the assessment of modeling and simulation in *products* generated by students and *processes* enacted by them, we also increase assessment fairness. For instance, research suggests that there tend to be discrepancies in achievement between racial groups (Traxler et al. 2018). However, in the laboratory or project-based courses, differences in achievement between these groups are not as common (Traxler et al. 2018). We acknowledge that focusing the assessment of modeling and simulation practices on higher-order skills may bring practical challenges. Such challenges include assessments being time-consuming and difficult to scale and requiring training for graders (Diefes-Dux et al. 2012). To balance feasibility and fairness, we recommend giving students multiple opportunities to demonstrate what they know and, at the same time, using a variety of assessment methods (Wiggins and McTighe 1997). Assessment methods can range from informal checks for understanding (e.g., participation and quizzes) to knowledge evaluation (e.g., tests and exams) to performance tasks (e.g., projects). In some instances, automated testing or assessments can assist in this process. For instance, in cases of simple models, automated assessments can evaluate for the correct solution, check for the use of the correct method, or evaluate the meeting of tolerances. We also recommend including a balance of collaborative and individual assessments. Students could work together in developing a computational model to be graded collaboratively but then have each student work on articulation or a reflection task individually. Examples of individual tasks could be to comment on the code, write the final report, use the jointly created models to execute different experiments, and submit an individual reflection assignment.

PEDAGOGICAL GUIDELINES FOR SUPPORTING MODELING AND SIMULATION

Once the learning objectives and corresponding assessment have been identified, the last step in the understanding by design framework is to determine the pedagogy to be followed, along with necessary instructional support. This section introduces a pedagogical model for guiding and supporting learners as they engage in modeling and simulation practices. The pedagogical model is the cognitive apprenticeship model, which has been derived from research in mathematics, reading, and writing education. The cognitive apprenticeship model (Collins, Brown, and Newman 1989, 3) proposes the design of learning environments that merge "the content being taught, the pedagogical methods employed, the sequencing of learning activities, and the sociology of learning." Although apprenticeship models are typically thought of in connection to physical or trade professions, the process by which individuals become proficient at integrating modeling and simulation practices involves many of the same elements of a traditional apprenticeship model (Sadler et al. 2010). The ultimate goal is that the instructor or instructional materials deliberately address the reasoning processes (i.e., the model-based reasoning processes) associated with performing a task or solving a problem, making them visible or explicit to the learner. Chapter 4 of this book further elaborates on the theoretical foundations of the cognitive apprenticeship model, its application to computation, modeling, and simulation teaching and learning, and future research directions.

Our approach for integrating computation, modeling, and simulation practices into the classroom follows the cognitive apprenticeship model guidelines to facilitate student learning and engagement. Specifically, the cognitive apprenticeship framework has been demonstrated to be effective in students' learning of important content and skills and their motivation and acceptance of course tasks and assignments. Accordingly, we followed Collins and Kapur's (2014) dimensions to support learning. The dimensions of the cognitive apprenticeship framework are *content*, referring to the types of knowledge required for expertise; *method*, referring to the pedagogical approach, learning strategies, or teaching methods used; *sequencing*, referring to designing the structure and the order of the tasks so as to optimize meaningful student engagement; and *sociology*, referring to the context within which learning experiences are situated via the application of skills to realistic problems (Collins and Kapur 2014). In the following sections, we describe each of the elements of the cognitive apprenticeship model, including an explanation of how each of them can be implemented in this context of modeling and simulation practice.

Content

The combination of domain knowledge with strategic knowledge has been referred to as the content dimension. Domain knowledge refers to specialized knowledge in specific disciplines. Strategic knowledge includes (1) heuristic strategies, which are tacit procedures that experts often use to solve common problems; (2) control strategies, including metacognitive strategies such as monitoring, evaluating, and overcoming difficulties, among others; and (3) learning strategies that deal with the identification of effective approaches for learning domain knowledge.

The content dimension is often accomplished inherently. Introducing modeling and simulation practices within STEM domains brings together multiple types of knowledge required for expertise. Specifically, combining domain knowledge with modeling and simulation skills can bring together problem-solving, experimentation, and computation skills. However, although this integration comes naturally, instructors need to design learning experiences that combine multiple types of knowledge and skills and at the same time help students recall their domain knowledge, facilitate its application throughout the modeling process, and engage them in experimentation and design processes. This means that the learning experience cannot finalize at the moment students complete the implementation of a model into an executable code. The learning experience should be extended so that students intentionally engage in validation and verification processes. And extended so that students, once they create and evaluate their model, then engage in experimentation practices to characterize a scientific phenomenon or engage in design processes to solve an engineering problem or design a system.

Method

The method dimension refers to teaching approaches designed to help students acquire integrated knowledge and skills through (1) modeling, where the instructor demonstrates how to perform a task; (2) coaching, including observation and facilitation at the moment students perform a task; (3) scaffolding, regarding supporting methods to help students perform a task; (4) articulation, consisting of instructors encouraging students to state their knowledge and thinking; (5) reflection, where instructors enable students to compare their performance with experts' approaches; and (6) exploration, consisting of instructors prompting students to solve problems on their own.

Different methods can be used to support learners in acquiring integrated knowledge and skills. Traditional methods in higher education include *modeling* and *coaching*, where the instructor demonstrates how to perform a task, and then students try it on their own, either as a homework assignment or in the laboratory as part of an experiment. *Articulation* is also common as students demonstrate and explain the knowledge learned in the form of project reports. However, there are two methods that are not often known or used by faculty: *scaffolding* and *reflection*. Scaffolding methods can be thought of as those strategies that can support the student when the faculty is not available to provide help (i.e., while solving a homework assignment). Scaffolding methods we have identified as highly effective include (1) the use of short video lectures explaining difficult concepts, (2) the use of worked-out examples (i.e., an expert solution to a problem) demonstrating difficult calculations or implementations of a particular function, (3) code snippets or templates of codes that can get students started with implementing their computational solutions, and (4) test cases that can provide students with opportunities to evaluate their solutions as they progress in their solution of modeling challenges (Vieira et al. 2020).

However, we would like to caution the reader. Making materials available is not enough; students often do not have the metacognitive skills to take advantage of these resources naturally. Therefore, checkpoints need to be put in place so students benefit from these resources. These checkpoints need to be translated into course credit that motivates students to meaningfully engage with the material. For instance, students can be prompted to take a quiz after watching a video lecture and get a score based on their answers. Students can also be provided with extra credit to comment on worked-out examples as a self-explanation strategy (Vieira et al. 2017).

Reflection methods can help students further connect their domain knowledge with modeling and simulation practice. Reflection is an active process that must be fostered by pedagogical design and supported through practice in the classroom (Jaiswal et al. 2021). Students can reflect on multiple aspects of their engagement with computation, modeling, and simulation. For instance, students can reflect on their experienced challenges and the problem-solving strategies that helped them overcome those challenges (Shaikh et al. 2015), or they can also reflect on how they evaluated and used evidence to support their findings as part of their final reports.

Sequencing

The sequencing dimension consists of the principles and procedures used to guide the ordering of the learning activities. Activities can be presented in three ways: (1) increasing level of complexity, from simple to complex; (2) increasing level of diversity, considering a widening variety of application areas; and (3) global before local skills, where learners first understand the relationship between concepts or principles before delving deeper into each of them (Collins, Brown, and Holum 1991). The sequencing principle can be adapted to provide explicit opportunities for students to engage in all stages of the modeling and simulation process. Specifically, complete class periods can be devoted so that students can analyze the problem to be solved and articulate an initial strategy. Students can submit their strategies to the instructors so they can also get specific guidance. Other class periods could be devoted to (1) the implementation of the algorithm into a form of executable code, (2) the evaluation of their models by providing them with test cases to compare results, and (3) the simulation of the model and interpretation of the findings.

Sociology

The sociology dimension relates to students learning skills in the context of their application to real-world challenges and aspects of the social environment. Characteristics affecting the sociology of learning environments include (1) learning opportunities, where students learn in the context of working on realistic problems; (2) communities of practice, where participants within the learning environment, such as a team, engage and communicate while acquiring skills; (3) motivational strategies, where tasks are related to a personal goal or interest; and (4) cooperation, where students work together in cooperative problem-solving. The sociology strategy that we have implemented in our research consists of contextualizing the programming assignments within authentic tasks (CTGV 1990). Contextualization can be used as a way to implement content and sociology by situating the learning experiences within authentic tasks occurring in real-life contexts. Therefore, as part of sociology, we concentrate on providing a balance between individual and student work.

Implementing a flipped-classroom approach is one technique that can help faculty balance individual and group work (Magana, Falk, and Reese 2013). Flipped-classroom involves the integration of active in-class activities combined with assigned work to be completed before and after the lecture (Abeysekera and Dawson 2015). Following this approach, students can get some preparation before coming to class and then engage in collaborative problem-solving during class time. Specifically, during the classroom sessions, students can work together in groups to discuss how they could approach a particular project and continue their discussions outside of the classroom. However, to make each student responsible, it is important that grading accounts for individual and group work. For instance, students can collaborate in defining and implementing a computational model collectively, but they work individually on their reports and submit their created artifacts individually.

3

CHAPTER 3 CONSISTS OF EXEMPLAR LEARNING DESIGNS THAT EMBED THE PRINCI-
ples and procedures described in chapter 2. To provide a common ground between all designs, each of them starts with an overview of the target audience and a lesson plan. The lesson plan provides a detailed description of the alignment between content, assessment, and pedagogy and the learning trajectory to be followed during the lesson. Some lessons may take a day, some may take a couple of weeks, and some are four-week-long implementations. Each learning design features a particular audience (i.e., K–12 students, first-year and advanced college students) and is delivered in a particular setting (i.e., in-class teaching, laboratory settings, capstone courses, and professional development). In addition, each is accompanied by an appendix that features (1) the indications of the actual project, (2) a solution of the project, (3) a detailed description of how the lesson was delivered, and (4) a rubric delineating assessment criteria. Each learning design concludes with individual reflections on lessons learned by each author during the implementation of the lesson.

DESIGNING FOR NOVICE LEARNERS
BY MICHAEL FALK

Introducing modeling and simulation practices into learning environments consisting primarily of novice learners is challenging for the instructor and students. The main reason is that computation, modeling, and simulation require the integration of multiple disciplines and practices that students are unfamiliar with. Specifically, students have to learn new programming concepts and combine those with scientific or engineering concepts and advanced mathematical models that may require solving complex equations. So the question is, How do we design modeling and simulation learning experiences for engineering students with minimal prior training in computing? And furthermore, What types of supports or scaffolding approaches are needed to assist students as they engage in these learning experiences? The first question will be answered in the first few sections of this learning design, while the second question will be answered through the lessons learned.

TIME-DEPENDENT PARTIAL DIFFERENTIAL EQUATION IMPLEMENTATION WITH MATLAB

Context, Population, and Learning Need

This lesson was designed for first-year engineering students enrolled in an introductory programming course. The programming course was a general gateway to computer science on the intermediate level in addition to providing a computing background for materials science and engineering students. This class was meant as a first introduction to applying algorithmic thinking and computer programming toward the solution of engineering and scientific problems. We used MATLAB as the programming environment. The learning objectives of the class were that the student would be able to (1) write MATLAB programs to execute well-defined algorithms, (2) design algorithms to solve engineering problems by breaking these into small tractable parts, and (2) model physical and biological systems by applying linear systems and ordinary and partial differential equations. The class size was 20 to 30 students.

Theoretical Grounding of the Learning Design

For the theoretical grounding of this learning experience, we used the How People Learn (HPL) framework (Bransford, Brown, and Cocking 2000). The HPL framework is composed of four intersecting components (or lenses): (1) knowledge-centered, where foundational knowledge skills and attitudes are the base core of the learning materials; (2) learner-centered, where learning materials connect students' prior knowledge and interests; (3) community-centered, where an appropriate learning environment is provided within and outside the classroom; and (4) assessment-centered, where learners are provided with multiple opportunities to represent their knowledge and receive feedback.

The course was *knowledge-centered* by combining concepts and practices of the introduction of programming principles and procedures within the context of the materials science discipline. At the same time, students reinforced and developed their computing concepts, methods, and practices through real-world applications of interest to students majoring in material science engineering and related fields. The course was *learner-centered* by applying an inverted classroom design method (Gannod, Burge, and Helmick 2008; Lage, Platt, and Treglia 2000), which provided learners with multiple opportunities for practice and feedback during class time. At the same time, the approach freed the instructor to use class time for collaborative activities in which students worked through exercises, making the course *community-centered*. The instructor helped students work through scaffolded programming activities as needed by continually monitoring student progress during class time. Specifically, students worked individually and in informal groups during class, solo or collaboratively, solving some brief programming exercises with short, interspersed instructor-led discussions of concepts that required clarification. The class as a whole then collectively constructed a master solution with instructor guidance. This provided opportunities to make the algorithm design and programming process visible and public. Students also discussed their approaches with classmates while working on projects. The course provided learners with multiple opportunities to demonstrate or apply their knowledge and receive feedback, thus making the course also *assessment-centered*. Specifically, students received feedback in real time from the professor and teaching assistant during class. In addition, students also received graded feedback on the project after scoring of the artifacts they generated (i.e., code, final report) with a rubric.

Problem Description and Learning Domain

The design of the project was centered on a modeling and simulation assignment to support research in devising minimally invasive and effective techniques to reverse ventricular fibrillation, an important medical issue. (Ventricular fibrillation is the state where the contraction of the lower heart chambers becomes disorganized and the heart is no longer able to adequately pump blood to the rest of the body. It is one of the most common causes of cardiac arrest.) Students were required to simulate the passage of an electrical pulse through the heart muscle. For this, the problem was modeled as a time-dependent partial differential equation.

While partial differential equations are typically advanced topics reserved for upper-division engineering courses requiring prior mastery of vector calculus and differential equations, in the context of modeling a physical or biological system, such equations can be motivated in intuitive ways that are accessible to the novice learner. We based this project on a numerical algorithm from the literature designed to efficiently model spiral waves, such as those that develop in heart tissue, using a two-variable system of reaction–diffusion equations (Barkley 1991). The resulting equations simulate the excitability of the tissue as well as the diffusion and response of the electrical potential. While complex to represent mathematically, the concept of diffusion itself is simple for students to grasp when presented as a mechanism by which each simulated grid point incrementally reverts to the mean of its nearest neighbors. Neumann boundary conditions with zero normal gradients were imposed by enforcing that the grid point values on the boundary are equal to the neighboring grid point adjacent to the boundary.

Lesson Plan

The following lesson plan (table 3.1) aligns the learning objectives with the design of the activity and its corresponding assessment. The project description, a possible project solution, and corresponding assessment rubrics are presented in appendix A.

Reflection and Lessons Learned

The implementation of the lesson started by having students individually and on their own time watch an online video that introduced the foundational knowledge, followed by an online quiz. Students then worked collaboratively during class, solving a series of short, preparatory programming exercises. These exercises took different forms, such as providing a working code to students and having them predict the program's outcome. Other exercises had students debug and fix a given code that was not working or implement a solution to generate the desired outcome. The class typically ended with a micro-challenge where students had to apply the concepts and skills learned during that class. Brainstorming sessions were facilitated by the instructor to elicit suggestions on how to approach the solution to each micro-challenge. After discussing potential

TABLE 3.1 *Lesson plan for the time-dependent partial differential equation project*

Instructor's name: Michael Falk	Discipline: Materials Science and Engineering	Course: Computation for Programing for MSE	Date: November 28, 2017

1. Name of the topic or unit:
Time-Dependent Partial Differential Equation Implementation

2. Learning objective (from the syllabus):
Use of iteration in the simulation of partial differential equations, representation of two-dimensional data in arrays, and boundary value problems.

3. Specific disciplinary learning objective(s) of the assignment/lab:
Students write MATLAB programs to solve mathematically well-defined problems.

4. Specific modeling and simulation practice(s):
Students implement simple computational models by creating discretized mathematical descriptions of an event or phenomenon using high-level programming languages or scientific computing software.
  • Model physical/biological systems are represented as a set of partial differential equations.

5. Assessment strategies and grading system:
A two-part project where the first part consists of the plan proposed by students to implement the solution, and the second part is the solution with the corresponding report.

Part I. Planning
  • Articulated strategy identifying the design of the solution, coding approach, testing strategy, and debugging approach (10%).

Part II. Solution and Documentation
  • Program execution is free of syntax errors and responds to specifications (25%).
  • Specification satisfaction is where the solution produces the correct output, and the output meets specifications (25%).
  • Well-structured and well-commented code (10%).
  • Evidence of validation of the solution, including test cases with justification and their evaluation (10%).
  • Evaluation of the solution under the lens of the disciplinary concepts (20%).

6. Guidance materials and resources such as laboratory manuals and project templates (see appendix A):
  • Instructor's online lectures
  • Worked examples for related exercises
  • Example of a plan for a generic coding problem
  • Test cases

7. Instrumentation and software tools:
  • MATLAB software

TABLE 3.1 *Continued*

8. Specific instructional events:
A. Teaching method (ways to promote the development of expertise; see appendix A)
Three main teaching methods will be used:
1. Coaching, where the instructors and TAs make themselves available during lectures, lab sessions, and extra office hours to provide feedback and individual consultations.
2. Scaffolding, provided in the following forms:
• Hints are embedded in the project description.
• Worked-out examples throughout the course provide students with approaches to solve parts of a bigger problem.
• A first iteration where students receive feedback from the instructor/TA on their strategy before engaging in the solution.
• Test cases that help students validate their solutions.
3. Articulation, where students are prompted to explain their solution via three different mechanisms:
• A preliminary strategy report where they structure their initial solution.
• In-code comments where they explain how they approached the algorithmic solution.
• A final report where they detail how they approached the problem and interpreted the solution under the disciplinary problem.
4. Reflection will be facilitated in two ways:
• Allow students to discuss their own solutions with their peers during the lecture and laboratory sessions.
• Have students compare their solutions against self-generated or instructor-provided test cases.
B. Sequencing of activities (ordering of learning activities; e.g., prelab, lecture, lab, homework)
The integration of the module will follow this sequence:
1. During class, the instructor introduces the theoretical background of the problem and how to model time-dependent partial differential equation boundary value problems.
2. Requirements for the code structure, the planning report, and the final report are established over the term.
3. During the laboratory session, students start working on their planning strategy. Students continue working on their strategy after class, and once done, they submit it for initial feedback.
4. Once feedback is received on their initial strategy, students continue to work on the challenge throughout the next week, in and outside of class. The instructor/TA provides continuous feedback.
5. After one week, students submit their solutions to the challenge (i.e., the MATLAB code) and the corresponding report.
C. Sociology (social and contextual characteristics of the learning environment; e.g., individual or teamwork)
Students will be allowed to discuss their solutions with their peers during class time, but the final solution and report should be produced, debugged, and submitted individually. Also, the instructor and TA will be available for one-on-one consultation.
9. Homework (if appropriate):
Students start the project during class time and work on it for one week.
10. General comments or observations:
N/A

approaches, students started their problem-solving processes, and when class time was not enough, students completed the micro-challenge outside the classroom. The instructor implemented this process on a weekly basis for two to three weeks. As students worked on the weeklong projects, feedback was provided via online discussion, during in-class workshops, and during office hours offered by the instructor and teaching assistant. A lesson concluded with a weeklong modeling and simulation project, like the one described in this lesson plan.

The first time we implemented this lesson, we learned that the course was perceived as challenging for students (Magana, Falk, and Reese 2013). However, as we designed, implemented, and iteratively revised this modeling and simulation project, we were able to identify the types of benefits and challenges experienced by the students. We also identified a collection of learning strategies that supported students' learning. One of the major challenges students experienced was mapping from a mathematical representation to an algorithmic and computational representation (Magana, Falk, et al. 2017). We also noticed that students did not fully engage with the modeling and simulation process. That is, students often planned and implemented their models but were not using them effectively to solve the actual engineering problem (Magana, Brophy, and Bodner 2012). Some students did not properly engage in the simulation aspect of the modeling and simulation process, while others did not enact important stages of the modeling process, such as validation and verification. We offer the following best practices for supporting student learning in this context to overcome these challenges.

We use worked-out examples to help students make meaningful connections between the disciplinary and computational content (Vieira, Yan, and Magana 2015). Worked-out examples are expert solutions to a problem. For the purposes of this project, such examples focused on helping students map from a mathematical equation to an algorithm. The examples were provided in the form of short videos and written explanations that were made available to students within the learning management system. However, as we implemented the worked-out examples, we noticed that students did not use the worked examples provided to them or did not engage meaningfully with the worked examples. For this, we implemented the use of in-code comments as a way for students to engage and self-explain the worked examples to themselves (Vieira et al. 2017; Vieira et al. 2019).

To gradually remove the support provided with the worked-out examples, we implemented an intermediate scaffolding approach consisting of providing templates of codes or code snippets. In this way, students could assemble part of the computational model by reusing code. These strategies gave students a starting point and allowed them to focus their efforts on the most critical components of the computational solution.

To engage students in model-based reasoning, we also provided guidance so students could enact each of the modeling and simulation stages (Magana et al. 2020). Recommended stages include (1) analyze the problem, (2) formulate a model, (3) implement and solve the model, (4) validate and verify the model, (5) interpret the solution, (6) report the model, and (7) maintain the model (Shiflet and Shiflet 2014). These stages can be combined for convenience, but it is recommended that at least (1) analyze and formulate the model, (2) implement and solve the problem, and (3) evaluate and interpret the solution are explicitly enacted. A simple approach to guide students through these stages was to provide project report templates. The report was organized into different stages, and a brief explanation of the expectations for each section was provided. Assessment rubrics also described the requirements and expected levels of performance for each stage.

A critical step often overlooked by faculty when implementing modeling and simulation practices is the validation and verification process. Although implementing these practices can be considered advanced skills, some support strategies can initiate students into the habit of validating and verifying their models. Such strategies include the instructor providing test cases with results so that students can compare their solutions. A second strategy is to provide students with data sets, theoretical models, or even other simulations.

Conclusion

Introducing modeling and simulation practices to novice learners is challenging because these practices require the integration of programming, disciplinary, and mathematical skills. Different forms of scaffolding can be implemented to support students in enacting modeling and simulation practices and help them overcome the most challenging steps of the modeling and simulation process. While worked-out examples with in-code commenting were useful supports, more research is needed to identify other possible struggles and corresponding supporting strategies.

DESIGNING FOR CAPSTONE COURSES BY JOSEPH LYON

When designing computation, modeling, and simulation challenges for capstone courses, one must consider a whole host of different issues than when designing for younger students. For example, students in a capstone course may have already encountered many of the concepts and skills needed to construct their models, and thus the process students must undergo involves connecting the dots from previous courses. Additionally, further knowledge transfer can be required as many students will have moved further toward expert-like practices and away from the novice practices they may have had earlier in the program. To add to the complexity, capstone students may vary widely in ability depending on how much they have grasped material in their previous years of undergraduate study. So the question now is, How do we help capstone students piece together the different previous learning experiences to transfer knowledge into new modeling and simulation contexts? And additionally, How do we account for the highly variable levels of ability we encounter when working with capstone students? These questions will be addressed in this learning design, along with example materials for practitioners and researchers to use alike.

MODELING HEAT TRANSFER AND STERILIZATION WITHIN A FOOD CANNING OPERATION

Context and Population

This learning design was developed for students enrolled in a capstone course. The students were enrolled in an engineering degree program focused on food and pharmaceutical processing, with a mix of students wanting to pursue graduate school and others focused on obtaining industry positions. The course was the first part of a two-part capstone design course. Consequently, in addition to the modeling activities during the semester, students had design groups that were working on a capstone project. The course met for six hours a week with two one-hour lectures and two two-hour lab periods. For each modeling project, students were expected to write a MATLAB script that modeled a real-world food or pharmaceutical process. Each modeling activity took a total of three to four weeks to complete, with four different activities across the semester. There were multiple learning objectives for the modeling activities where the students were able to (1) describe real-world systems with mathematical models, (2) convert mathematical models into computational models in MATLAB, and (3) interpret the output of computational models within the real-world context of the modeling problem.

Theoretical Grounding of the Learning Design

Two primary frameworks were used to guide the pedagogical design of this project. The first framework is productive failure, which suggests that students learn to transfer knowledge into ill-structured problem contexts by being pushed to the point of failure or an impasse (Kapur 2010). Productive failure prescribes very little instruction prior to the intervention by encouraging students to explore the problem space on their own (Kapur and Bielaczyc 2012). In our context with capstone students, this is a helpful framework in that many of the students had received most of the information they needed in prior classes and just needed to integrate it, as opposed to first-year or novice learners, who may require much more instruction prior to beginning work on a task. Additionally, productive failure design encourages problems to be ill-structured, which can include giving students problems that have multiple solutions or vague or partially unknown parameters and requiring them to make assumptions about the problem space (Kapur 2010). In our classroom, this played out by giving students a problem that required them to model a canning sterilization operation. Students received the necessary instruction on topics such as heat transfer, reaction kinetics, and finite difference modeling. However, this task required them to pull these knowledge domains together, and little instruction was provided on this aspect before they began to plan their solutions. Additionally, the problem given had multiple variables containing ranges, multiple missing variables students would need, extraneous information and values, and many layers of assumptions to accomplish.

Additionally, the modeling projects were structured using a model-eliciting activity (MEA) framework, which has been studied extensively in engineering and broader

STEM contexts (Diefes-Dux et al. 2004; Lesh et al. 2011; Lyon and Magana 2021). The MEA framework follows six principles for designing modeling activities (Diefes-Dux et al. 2004):

Model-construction principle: The activity should result in a mathematically focused model.

Reality principle: The activity should be set within a realistic and meaningful setting.

Self-assessment principle: The activity should be set up in a way to allow students to evaluate how they are thinking about the modeling problem.

Model-documentation principle: The activity should require students to document their work at each stage of the problem-solving process.

Construct shareability principle: The activity should allow students to create solutions that are transferable to other solution spaces.

Effective prototype principle: The activity has students create a simple but effective solution.

These six principles were used to create the artifacts needed for the modeling project. The problem was set within a highly realistic engineering scenario (reality principle). At each stage in the process, students filled out project templates (model-documentation principle). The project had an activity built in that had students evaluate how good their model was, what they could have done differently, and in what other scenarios they might use this type of model (self-assessment principle and construct shareability principle). And finally, students were asked to make and defend assumptions of their model and create a finite difference model of the process they were evaluating (model-construction principle and effective prototype principle).

Problem Description and Learning Domain

The problem was situated as a modeling and simulation problem where students were asked to model the sterilization of food products on a canning line. The students were placed in the situation of an engineering consulting group that had been approached by a systems engineer in the food industry to model the heat transfer and sterilization of various food products as they are exposed to heat in a retort operation. This is a common unit operation within the food industry—one that is critical to food safety—that students will likely encounter when they enter industry careers. Students needed to integrate knowledge from heat transfer in biological materials, the reaction kinetics of microbial agents and food nutrients, and finite difference modeling of differential equations to effectively solve the challenge posed to them.

Lesson Plan

The following lesson plan (table 3.2) outlines the specific details of the learning activity implemented within this context. Corresponding rubrics, handouts, and student templates are presented in appendix B.

TABLE 3.2 *Lesson plan for the food sterilization project*

Instructor's name: Joseph Lyon	Discipline: Biological and Food Process Engineering	Course: Transport Operations in Food and Biological Systems II
1. Name of the topic or unit: Food Sterilization		
2. Learning objective (from the syllabus): Analyze common unit operations in the food and pharmaceutical industries.		
3. Specific disciplinary learning objective(s) of the assignment/lab: • Apply numerical modeling techniques of food processing systems in real-world contexts. • Analyze complex heat transfer scenarios.		
4. Specific modeling and simulation practice(s): The following are modeling and simulation-specific practices to be assessed as learning objectives (LO): • Students are able to identify useful data and justify its use. • Students are able to convert mathematical representations of information into appropriate computational structures and justify their choice. • Students are able to construct computational models from identified information and develop computational structures. • Students are able to interpret modeling output in relation to problem context and other student solutions. • Students are able to discuss the limitations of their model and additional applications of the model.		
5. Assessment strategies and grading system: Assignments will be graded following the rubric provided in appendix B. There are five deliverables from the activity: • *Planning the model template (15%, LO1):* Students will work in teams to begin mapping out how they will do the activity. • *MATLAB coding template (30%, LO2):* Students will work individually to create the mapped-out model in the MATLAB programming environment. • *Building the model template (30%, LO3):* Students will work individually to fill out a building the model template in which they explain their design decisions, assumptions, and limitations of their model. • *Evaluating the model template (15%, LO4):* Students will fill out a note-taking template while they meet with other students to discuss how their models differed. • *Reflecting on the model template (10%, LO5):* Students individually fill out a reflection template in which they think about the solution process and what they may do differently next time.		
6. Guidance materials and resources such as laboratory manuals and project templates: Students will be provided with multiple documents before the activity, all found in appendix B. The problem statement overviews a processing plant that has reached out to your engineering team to solve line issues and the realistic MEA-inspired scenario. The MATLAB coding template gives overarching structure to the code as well as explains how teams should structure comments within the code. Templates are provided for each stage of the activity.		

TABLE 3.2 *Continued*

7. Instrumentation and software tools: Access to MATLAB software will be needed for the programming portion of the assignment, as well as access to word processing software.
8. Specific instructional events: *A. Teaching method* The teaching methods employed in this learning intervention are guided by the principles of the productive failure framework. In this framework, instructors are encouraged to create an environment with the following pedagogical qualities (Kapur and Bielaczyc 2012): • Instructors should aim to create an environment where problem space exploration is encouraged. For example, if a student is stuck and looking for a way forward, instructors should push them to think of a different way to set up the problem or different ways to think about an aspect of the problem. • Instructors should shy away from emphasizing one correct way to solve the problem but rather stress to students that there is no one correct solution to the problem (even though there might be better or worse solutions). • Whenever students mention multiple solution pathways, instructors should encourage them to consider the differences between the solutions and why one might be more limited or useful than another. *B. Sequencing of activities* A four-week sequence is required to cover all parts of the learning activity. *Week 0:* The instructor gives a brief intro to the problem the students will be solving (~15 minutes). Students work together in groups of four to fill out the planning model template (~90 minutes). By the end of the class, students should each have filled out the planning model template. *Weeks 0–3:* Students work individually outside of class to build their planned-out model using MATLAB software. Students are welcome and encouraged to make changes to their plan if needed. At the end of this period, students are expected to turn in a completed building the model template and associated MATLAB files. During this time, the instructor will give three lectures on the topic: • Lecture 1: A review of heat transfer in food systems. • Lecture 2: A review of reaction kinetics of microbial systems. • Lecture 3: A review of finite difference modeling. *Week 3:* Students meet together in groups to evaluate their created models. Students meet together in their planning groups again and rotate around to meet with other groups of students from the class. During this time, students take notes to answer key questions, such as how their models differ and how other students' models work. *Weeks 3–4:* Students individually fill out a reflection template outside of class, considering what they would change about their model and what other applications their model might have. *C. Sociology (social and contextual characteristics of the learning environment, e.g., individual or teamwork)* Activity includes both group and individual components to the problem. Both the planning and evaluation phases are done as a group to spark creativity and new ways of thinking about the problem. The model phase is performed individually so that each student is personally exposed to the programming environment and solving the problem. Finally, the reflection phase is done individually to help students work on metacognitive skills, which are largely individual in nature.

Reflection and Lessons Learned

The first time this lesson was implemented was through a single modeling project over the course of the semester. The project allowed students to tie together various areas of knowledge they had previously learned in class, implemented through a programming context. The specific context of the project was the sterilization of food materials. The project started in a lab session of the course, in an open classroom, with students sitting around tables working together on their planning assignments on their computers. Instructors pulled up the assignment documents on projectors situated around the classroom for all students to see. The teaching team walked around the classroom during the two-hour planning session, answering questions and prompting student thought. While the building phase of the model was primarily done at home by the students individually, they again met with these teams three weeks later in the same classroom. The students evaluated their models with the teams they planned, then rotated to other tables to meet with students from three other planning teams. After the evaluation phase, students individually turned in a reflection report on their models. At the end of the project, students gave feedback on the intervention via a survey.

The evidence and results indicated that the intervention got students to practice computational thinking while solving these complex modeling challenges (Lyon and Magana 2021; Lyon, Magana, and Streveler 2022). Students demonstrated complex forms of abstraction, algorithmic thinking, and evaluation practices while solving the sterilization challenge. Additionally, students reported multiple benefits to the intervention, such as having a real-life simulated challenge and a hands-on learning project (Lyon, Magana, and Okos 2019). Students largely believed that the building and evaluating phases of the activity were the most helpful, while the reflection phase of the activity was largely acknowledged by the students as the least beneficial (Lyon, Magana, and Okos 2019).

The subsequent iterations of the implementation had multiple modeling projects in this format over the course of the semester. This allowed students to get into a pattern of how the modeling process worked, going from planning to building to evaluating and, finally, to reflecting. While productive failure was integrated to make students reach an impasse, more introductory instruction was given in subsequent semesters to alleviate some of the frustration and increase students' perceived benefit to the initial planning phase (Lyon, Magana, and Okos 2019). Subsequent semesters also included a scaffolding program called MATLAB Live Scripts, which allowed instructors to integrate the programming template with the report template for the project. Our results indicated that by doing so, the students significantly felt more comfortable with programming by the end of the modeling project and felt that the scaffolding through MATLAB Live was extremely beneficial (Lyon et al. 2020).

Finally, integrating reflection not only at the end of the activity but throughout the activity was implemented in subsequent iterations. Not only is reflection beneficial to students in building key metacognitive skills, but it also needs to be integrated so that students are reflecting before, during, and after any project (Ertmer and Newby 1996). Our subsequent iterations of the intervention have integrated reflection throughout to address low student perceived benefit to the reflection process, but also so that students have more opportunity to practice their reflection skills throughout the semester. Future interventions should work to integrate reflection earlier in the degree program so that by the capstone course, this practice is significantly integrated into students' workflow.

Conclusion

Upper-division engineering courses provide prime opportunities for instructors to integrate modeling and simulation projects into the engineering curriculum. Our learning design showed that students were able to use and practice their computational thinking skills and proved to be what many students are hungry for in the classroom: a realistic, hands-on learning project that simulates what they will be doing in industry. Future efforts should include more room for student reflection and an appropriate introduction to the materials in order to alleviate students' perceived drawbacks to the intervention.

DESIGNING FOR LEARNING IN THE LABORATORY BY HAYDEN FENNELL

The undergraduate laboratory is an ideal setting in which to introduce students to modeling and simulation practice. While computation is beginning to make its way into more and more standard STEM courses, the potential of using computation in the laboratory has been underutilized. Historically seen as an opportunity for students to gain "hands-on" experience with the subject matter, traditional labs often focus on physical experimentation and data collection. Alternatively, some labs have been converted into entirely computational labs in which students run simulations to demonstrate the concepts being learned in class (Fennell et al. 2019, Landau 2006). However, we propose a more balanced approach to in-lab computation that uses both physical experimentation and computational simulation to solidify student learning of disciplinary material through multiple representations of the same system.

MODELING FUNDAMENTAL MECHANICS IN PHYSICS LABS WITH VPYTHON

Context, Population, and Learning Need

Our design for hybrid computational/experimental physics labs was implemented in the context of Modern Mechanics, a large institution's first-year physics course. While the course focuses on the fundamentals of classical mechanics, the laboratory component of the course implements programming problems to introduce students to basic computational concepts in physics. The coding portions of the labs utilized VPython (an extension of the Python language) as the programming language. Students wrote and ran their code using GlowScript, an online VPython compiler. Labs were separated into three components: (1) physical experiment, (2) computational simulation, and (3) comparison and reflection questions. After setting up and collecting data on the physical experiment for each week, the students would use a provided VPython template to construct a computational model of the experiment they had just performed. Students would then be presented with a series of questions asking them to discuss the differences and similarities between the two sets of results.

Although this physics course is offered through the physics department, it is one of the required courses in the institution's first-year engineering program. Students in the first-year engineering program receive two MATLAB courses during their first year. However, most students tend to take the physics course during their first semester, meaning that for many, this is one of their first experiences with programming. Overall, students in this physics course tend not to have much coding experience, particularly in the context of code being used to model disciplinary problems. A primary benefit of introducing computational concepts in the laboratory environment is that it offers students a chance early in the curriculum to use computational tools to model a phenomenon as it is being studied through traditional experiments. In other words, the direct application of the computational methods is made clear each week due to the immediacy and hands-on nature of laboratory activities.

Theoretical Grounding of the Learning Design

The physics lab was developed using Kolb's theory of experiential learning (Kolb, Boyatzis, and Mainemelis 2011). Experiential learning theory (ELT) is a constructivist learning model that posits personal experience as the most central element of the learning process. Unlike cognitivist and behaviorist models, ELT suggests that all learning is based on experience and that the ways in which people interact with and process their own experiences influence how they learn. Experiential learning, therefore, acts as a sort of synthesis of the previous constructivist work introduced by Dewey, Lewin, and Piaget (Kolb, Boyatzis, and Mainemelis 2011). The ELT model suggests that there are two related processes of interfacing with experience during learning: grasping experience and transforming experience. The model of grasping experience consists of two related mental processes: concrete experience and abstract conceptualization. The model of transforming experience also consists of two related processes: reflective observation and active experimentation. Together, these two models of grasping and transforming experience intersect into a four-part process in which a learner (1) has an experience and (2) takes time to reflect and think about what they have observed, which allows for (3) the distillation of the experience into key elements of an abstract conceptualization of the experience before (4) participating in active experimentation to create further experiences, thereby repeating the process to refine their understanding of the phenomenon or experience (and thus generate new knowledge). This learning cycle makes up the basis of the ELT framework upon which instructional approaches can be built.

Our physics lab curriculum leverages the ELT framework through a laboratory structure that requires students to engage with this cycle in each hybrid experimental/computational lab. By performing the physical experiment at the beginning of each lab activity, students gain concrete experience of the studied phenomenon. After performing the experiment, students engage in *reflective observation* through analysis of the collected data, answering questions about the results, and making sense of the outcomes of their experiment. This is then followed by a computational simulation of the phenomenon under study, which models the key components of the physical experiment and encourages *abstract conceptualization* of the core elements of the phenomenon. Finally, students are led into *active experimentation* by being asked to make changes to the computational model to visualize different possible system configurations. Students then compare their results with the results of their experiment to draw conclusions about the accuracy of the models and experimental setups. While each lab session represents only one complete cycle of the ELT model, this cycle is repeated each week, exposing students to many related phenomena modeled with very similar code. The labs, when taken together, can be thought of as an extended version of the ELT cycle that lasts over the course of the entire semester rather than a single activity that gives students opportunities to iterate through the cycle multiple times in one sitting.

Problem Description and Learning Domain

Over the course of the semester, the physics lab covered a number of different topics. The details of the progression of content are provided in figure 3.1. Here we will discuss a module of three related labs covering the mechanics of objects under different types of acceleration: Lab 2, Lab 3, and Lab 8. These three labs comprised the lab course's discussion of simple linear motion. Labs 2 and 3 involved cart and track experiments in which carts were accelerated down a flat track, while Lab 8 focused on the air resistance and drag forces of a falling object. Each of the labs was modeled in VPython as a finite difference problem. This is a common solution method for time-dependent models in which each iteration of the program loop calculates the current results using

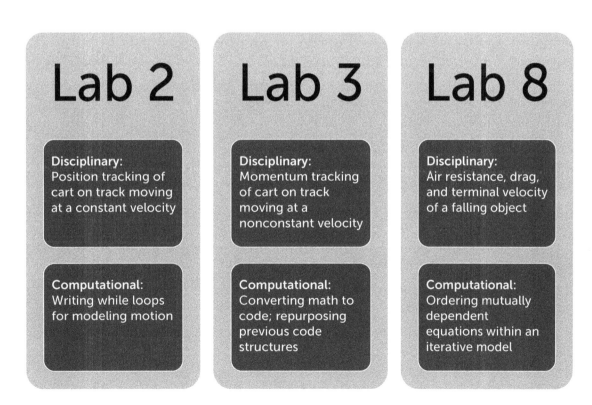

FIGURE 3.1 Disciplinary and computational content is covered in each lab within the linear motion module.

the results from the previous iteration of the loop as initial value inputs (i.e., updating the position/velocity of a moving object over time). These labs primarily covered concepts of selecting appropriate time step size, loops, and conditional logic. VPython code for the visual simulation setup was provided to the students in the form of a VPython template. Students were primarily responsible for defining variables, setting up calculations, and determining the order of equations in the loop that ran each program. The commands for plotting the simulation outputs were also provided in the template to reduce the learning load (given that the lab sessions were only two hours and also contained a complete physical experiment). The materials provided to the students for this lab module are provided in full in appendix C.

Lesson Plan

The following lesson plan (table 3.3) aligns the learning objectives with the design of the activity and its corresponding assessments. The project description for Labs 2, 3, and 8, as well as the code templates provided to the students and the corresponding assessment rubrics, are presented in appendix C.

TABLE 3.3 *Lesson plan for the Newtonian mechanics, linear motion/acceleration project*

Instructor's name: Hayden Fennell	Discipline: First-Year Engineering and Physics	Course: Modern Mechanics
1. Name of the topic or unit: Newtonian Mechanics, Linear Motion/Acceleration		
2. Learning objective (from the syllabus): Use loops to model motion iteratively in VPython; measure 1D position, velocity, and acceleration (Labs 2 and 3); use the drag coefficient and other parameters from the physical experiment to create a VPython model of the falling object (Lab 8); connect physical experiment and the VPython model		
3. Specific disciplinary learning objective(s) of the assignment/lab: Students modify provided VPython code templates to create a functioning model of the physical experiment performed in the first half of the lab.		
4. Specific modeling and simulation practice(s): Students modify/create simple VPython programs that leverage loops to model the motion of objects using an iterative finite difference approach.		
5. Assessment strategies and grading system: Each lab is assessed for disciplinary (i.e., physical experiment) performance and computational (VPython program) performance according to the rubrics found in appendix C. Scoring is less formal due to the more relaxed lab setting and low portion of the overall course grade (10%).		
6. Guidance materials and resources such as laboratory manuals and project templates: • Guided lab worksheets/manuals • VPython code templates		
7. Instrumentation and software tools: • VPython (Python 2.7 add-on package) delivered via GlowScript online programming environment (http://www.glowscript.org)		

TABLE 3.3 *Continued*

8. Specific instructional events: *A. Teaching method: use-modify-create framework (Lee et al. 2011)* The UMC framework is a computational scaffolding method in which students are first exposed to fully functioning software/programs that they *use* to solve a problem. Then they are asked to *modify* code that is incomplete or incorrect in order to use the code to solve a problem. Finally, students are asked to *create* code of their own once they have gained experience using and modifying steps. This process can be repeated whenever new disciplinary or computational concepts are introduced in order to help students develop an integrated body of knowledge and skills. *B. Lab activities (linear motion module)* *Lab 2:* VPython loops tutorial and simple cart and track experiment (recording position data as cart moves at constant velocity). Completed simulation code is provided to students who must alter initial parameters to produce results aligned with their experiment. (Use phase) *Lab 3:* Similar cart and track experiment with fan attachment to provide constant acceleration to the cart. Students must revise the code provided in Lab 2 to reflect the new experimental context. (Modify phase) *Lab 8:* Experiment involving air resistance of falling object and the calculation of drag coefficient from experimental data. Students must change parameters and add equations in the current locations in a provided template to produce a functioning simulation of the experiment. (Modify phase)
9. Homework (if appropriate): N/A
10. General comments or observations: It may be noted that the linear motion module discussed in point 8 does not include any examples of the *create* phase of the UMC framework. This portion of the framework was excluded intentionally due to the strict two-hour time limit of each lab session and the generally low experience with programming of the student population. Given the limitations of the lab setting, the *modify* phase felt like a strong enough challenge for the students during the fall 2018 semester. However, more *create* challenges were included in the following semesters, given the students' overall favorable performance in the labs in fall 2018 (see the section "Reflection and Lessons Learned" for more details).

Reflection and Lessons Learned

Overall, the first semester of implementation was very successful. Aside from a few logistical challenges involved in coordinating with the team of TAs responsible for running the labs and for catching and updating small issues with the code templates as students found them, the content of the labs themselves seemed quite approachable to the students. Performance results from the first semester of the hybrid labs were promising and showed that students were generally able to successfully engage with the lab material without too much trouble. The results of a thematic analysis found several themes of learning benefits within a selection of students' responses to questions on the in-class lab worksheets (Fennell et al. 2019). The themes of learning benefits are described in table 3.4.

The thematic analysis also intended to identify themes of challenge that students faced during the semester. However, very few instances of challenges were identified in the students' responses. Only two distinct challenges occurred across more than one

TABLE 3.4 *Themes of students' perceptions regarding learning benefits*

Theme of Benefit	Description
VPython basics	Evidence of understanding the basic functionality of programming in VPython (i.e., assigning variables, conditional logic/operators, vector math operations, etc.).
Iterative modeling	Evidence of understanding that computational models can do the same calculation repeatedly (i.e., using loops to simulate motion).
Step size and accuracy	Evidence of understanding the importance of step size within a model and its relationship to accuracy and precision.
Models are ideal and make assumptions	Evidence of understanding that models differ from the real world and make key assumptions and judgments about reality.
Models are contextually dependent	Evidence of understanding that models are representative of a particular context and must be updated if moved to new contexts.

student, each of which appeared only twice in total. These two challenges were (1) *model is truth*, in which students regard the model as the "true" physical representation rather than the data collected in the real-world physical experiment, and (2) *misidentification of code function*, in which a student leaves an in-code comment that incorrectly describes what a line of code does. While this is heartening in the sense that it shows that the hybrid lab material was generally not overwhelming for students, it also suggests that the initial implementation of the labs may have been over-scaffolded and that students are capable of meeting higher demands during the lab sessions. This over-scaffolding effect was likely the result of a more cautious "pilot" approach to the first deployment of the new hybrid material due to the extremely high enrollment in the class as a prerequisite for other required classes.

Since very few useful themes of challenges were identified during the thematic analysis, an additional round of thematic analysis was performed on the lab worksheets and code templates themselves. This time the goal was to identify any notable issues with the structure of the activities that may have led to the lack of observable challenges from the students. The themes related to limitations were also organized into several umbrella categories of issues to improve in the next iteration, as described in table 3.5.

These themes of limitation led to reflection on the learning activities and suggestions for improvement in future implementations of similar content. The first and most prominent issue with the responses to the lab activities was an overall lack of reflective description in students' answers. Reflection questions that encouraged students to make connections between the two portions of each lab were included each week, but answers were generally short and to the point. While students were prompted to make comparisons between their experimental and computational results, many settled on simple (and sometimes superficial) responses that technically addressed the question without saying very much. In general, it seems that students did not feel that extensive or detailed explanations were required to address the prompt, leaving very few instances of students clearly demonstrating their understanding (or lack of understanding)

TABLE 3.5 *Themes of students' perceptions regarding learning limitations*

Theme of Limitation	Description
Narrowly worded question/prompt	Question/prompt in lab activity was worded in a way that produced unanimous student responses (i.e., the question was too direct or had very few possible answers).
Lack of meaningful reflection/ explanation	Lab activities did not provide enough opportunity (or space) for meaningful reflection from the student.
Abbreviated answers	Students provided answers that were technically correct but too short to be informative or reflective of learning.
Incomplete answer to the compound question	Students did not fully answer prompts containing multiple questions.
Poor in-code commenting	Students did not provide useful comments on their coding templates, despite instructions to do so in each lab.

of the computational concepts being discussed. The wording of the questions in future implementations of the lab material was updated to be more explicit about what students were supposed to be reflecting on, rather than simple "why or why not" prompts that are often overlooked. A second, related observation about how to improve the labs was a more straightforward fix: avoid compound questions. A large amount of potential information was lost in the lab handouts due to students not fully answering questions with multiple parts. Many students would answer the first portion of a question and move on to the next, ignoring the more critical interpretation components of the question prompt. While this phenomenon has been identified and discussed by other authors (Mackillop, Parker-Swift, and Crossley 2011), we were not anticipating the extent to which it would be a problem in the hurried lab environment. Future implementations of the lab have broken all multipart questions into individual prompts to encourage students to fully engage with each question. While this issue is not exclusive to modeling contexts, it is one to be especially aware of when the activity is already asking students to split their attention across multiple areas of focus (in a hybrid experimental/computational lab assignment, for instance).

On the more modeling-specific side of things, there were two limitations that we feel can be addressed with the design of the labs. The first suggestion is that while scaffolding should still be removed gradually, it can be reduced more quickly than in the initial implementation. The first round of implementation of the labs maintained a sort of base level of scaffolding throughout the semester, providing students with fairly detailed code templates for each lab. The analysis of student performance in the labs suggests that students adapt quickly to modifying previous code for use in new (but related) settings and that less guidance is needed in the code templates later in the semester. In short, more activities from the *create* portion of the use-modify-create framework should be incorporated into the activities in order to see where students are still struggling or where any misconceptions may lie. If lack of expertise is still a concern in a setting where students are not exposed to much computational content, the *modify* step can also be leveraged more heavily as a method for removing scaffolding without leaving novice learners completely on their own. For example, implementations of the hybrid lab content after the fall 2018 pilot have students reusing and updating their cart and track code from Lab 3 in a later lab on air resistance of a falling object rather than simply providing the students with a content-appropriate template. The students, therefore, must make substantial changes to the code that border on creation levels of complexity but are supported by the fact that they are not simply presented with a blank text file (the assumption being that at least some of what they have done must be reusable in the current context if they are being instructed to use it).

A further issue faced on the computational side of things was that students tended not to leave very detailed in-code comments in their submitted programs, despite being asked to do so in each lab. When comments were left at all, they tended to be brief and mechanistic, often simply describing the programming function of a particular line rather than how it relates to the disciplinary problem (e.g., simply typing "position update equation" next to the line that updates the variable named position). Of the complications encountered with the labs, this was the most prominent. Many students simply stopped including comments in their code after the third or fourth lab, presumably due to time constraints or the students not seeing the value in leaving comments on things they feel they already know. Although unfortunate, this is not a surprising issue to encounter, given the general lack of programming exposure that many of the physics students had prior to the course. As such, it is worth considering how to ensure that students are shown the value of in-code commenting as a tool both for thinking through a problem and for communicating their understanding of a problem to other users of the code (Vieira et al. 2020). When it comes to assessment, it is especially important that students leave detailed comments that tie the code to the disciplinary content, as it is often the only real way of determining how well a student understands the code in lieu of a detailed ex post facto report about each lab assignment. Finding ways to encourage students to leave meaningful comments is an ongoing concern for future implementations of the lab material.

Conclusion

On the whole, the implementations of the hybrid labs have been a success, and any initial reservations about the hybrid material being "too much" for students to handle in a two-hour lab session have been assuaged by several semesters of successful implementation. The students have demonstrated that working with computational content in their labs is useful to their learning without detracting from the overall content of the labs. While the results from the first implementation showed that students were generally not overloaded by the labs, the quality of the responses to many questions indicated that more specificity was needed in the lab worksheet questions to encourage students to more fully demonstrate their knowledge. Finding ways for students to show their understanding of computational concepts in a disciplinary-focused course is an ongoing challenge for discipline-based computing that will greatly benefit from further work in a variety of other contexts.

DESIGNING FOR K–12 SETTINGS
BY CAMILO VIEIRA

Computational practices, including modeling and simulation, are now being integrated into K–12 curricula around the globe. Countries such as the United Kingdom (Department for Education 2013), the United States (CSTA 2017), and Australia (ACARA n.d.; Yadav, Stephenson, and Hong 2017) have now established a curriculum or a set of guidelines to integrate computational thinking from early childhood. Bringing these complex topics into the classroom is not an easy task for middle and high school teachers. They are often not prepared with the knowledge and skills to design these learning environments, which are actually complex for students and require appropriate scaffolding. Moreover, it is important to make this knowledge accessible and relevant for students, who may think that computer programming is only for computer scientists. The learning design that follows describes a learning environment that supports students in modeling the spread of infectious diseases. This learning environment also provides scaffolding to student learning using an interactive tutorial.

MODELING THE SPREAD OF AN INFECTIOUS DISEASE

Context and Population

This learning design models the spread of infectious diseases such as COVID-19 using a simple epidemiological model called Susceptible-Infected-Recovered (SIR). We propose that this learning design can be implemented in 10th grade, when students have developed some basic skills of programming and understand algebra concepts, such as variables. Before introducing this learning design within the K–12 level, we conducted a comparison of existing K–12 computing curricula in different countries, including the United Kingdom (Department for Education 2013), the United States (CSTA 2017), and Australia (ACARA n.d.). We identified that initially the learning outcomes should be very concrete and context-independent (e.g., using loops to automate a repetitive task) and start in the early years of middle school. Then, instructors can build toward more open-ended context-dependent learning outcomes (e.g., design, use, and evaluate computational abstractions that model the state and behavior of real-world problems and physical systems; Department of Education 2013).

Theoretical Grounding of the Learning Design

Cognitive load theory (CLT) informs this learning design, as it scaffolds student learning following a use-modify-create progression to reduce the cognitive loads. CLT suggests a cognitive architecture that comprises a working memory (WM) and a long-term memory (LTM) (Sweller, van Merriënboer, and Paas 2019). The WM is limited in time and space, while the LTM is vast. When we learn a new concept or skill, we load these new pieces of information into our WM and try to make sense of the information using the schemata we have organized in our LTM. Since our WM is limited in space (i.e., it can only process between four and seven chunks of information at a time), complex learning processes such as computer programming may overload it, affecting our learning process.

Computer programming is a complex skill to learn (Mselle and Twaakyondo 2012; Vieira et al. 2019). Novice programmers need to learn simultaneously about algorithm design, the programming language syntax and semantics, the program's goal, and how the computer processes information. Hence, to support student learning of computer programming, it is important to reduce extraneous cognitive loads. While some strategies have focused on reducing the number of things students need to learn (e.g., using block-based programming to avoid syntax errors), others suggest focusing on developing early schemata by scaffolding the student learning process (Vieira et al. 2017). A way to scaffold the learning process could be via worked examples. A worked example is an expert's solution to a problem. When novice learners actively explore a worked example, they may identify basic concepts and strategies that will enable them to engage in problem-solving activities later. Once the learner starts developing such schemata, they prefer to try to solve problems on their own instead of studying someone else's work (Vieira et al. 2019). In the context of computational thinking and programming education, researchers and educators suggest the progression of use-modify-create to scaffold the student learning process (Vieira et al. 2023). In this progression, students first actively explore an example (i.e., use), predict the outcome, and self-explain or explain to each other. Then, students work on an activity to make some change or extension to the example program (i.e., modify). Once the students have developed the required schemata, they work on a challenge (i.e., create) through an iterative cycle of create-test-analyze-refine until they find a solution to the problem.

Problem Description and Learning Domain

This lesson plan models the spread of a disease using a traditional epidemiological model called Susceptible-Infected-Recovered (SIR), which is used to depict how a disease (e.g., COVID-19) spreads within a given population. The SIR model assumes that each individual can be in one of four states:

Susceptible (S): Individuals who have not been infected with the disease, so they are susceptible to being infected within a given probability of disease transmission (i.e., transmission rate) and an average number of contacts per person per time (i.e., contact rate).

Infected (I): Individuals who are infected and can be infectious to others. There is a probability of both recovery and death associated with leaving this state.

Recovered (R): Individuals who were already infected but are now recovered. These individuals cannot be reinfected since they have developed antibodies. (*Note:* This is not necessarily the case for COVID-19, as the evidence about it is inconclusive at this point, but this is the case for other diseases and an assumption of this model.)

Deceased (D): Individuals who were infected and died as a result of the disease.

To identify how many people will move from one state to another, we use the following variables:

Contact rate: Average number of contacts per person per day.
Transmission rate: Probability of disease transmission when a susceptible person comes in contact with an infected person.
Recovery rate: Probability of recovery after being infected.
Mortality rate: Probability of dying after being infected.
Recovery time: Average number of days that the disease stays in the body.

To simulate this model, we need to compute the number of new infections, recoveries, and deaths per day and then update the number of susceptible, infected, recovered, and deceased as follows:

NewInfections: Infected × Contact rate × (Susceptibles / Total population) × Transmission rate
NewRecoveries: Infected × Recovery rate / Recovery time
NewDeaths: Infected × Mortality rate / Recovery time
Susceptibles: Susceptibles – NewInfections
Infected: Infected + NewInfections – (NewRecoveries + NewDeaths)
Recovered: Recovered + NewRecoveries
Deceased: Deceased + NewDeaths

As one may expect, there are some variables that we can manipulate and see the effects on the number of infected people and the number of deaths. For instance, closing public events and banning large gatherings of people may decrease the *contact rate*, which has a direct effect on the number of new infections and the number of deaths. Likewise, if doctors find effective treatments for the disease, we may have a lower *mortality rate*, which will reduce the number of deaths. The plots in figure 3.2 show the results from a simulation configured for a city of one million people over the course of 365 days. As you may have already identified, the three figures correspond to three different scenarios where the recovery rate and the contact rate were modified.

Lesson Plan

The following lesson plan (table 3.6) aligns the learning objectives with the design of the activity and its corresponding assessments. The project description, the code handout provided to the students, and the corresponding assessment rubrics are presented in appendix D.

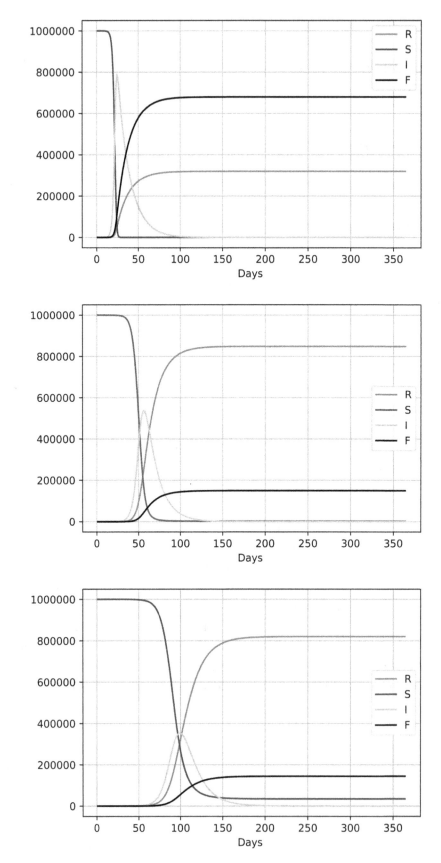

FIGURE 3.2 Three scenarios of the SIR model represent the four possible states over a year (365 days): Recovered (R), Susceptible (S), Infected (I), and Deceased (F).

TABLE 3.6 *Lesson plan for modeling the spread of an infectious disease project*

Instructor's name: Camilo Vieira	Discipline: Natural Sciences	Course: 10th Grade Science
1. Name of the topic or unit: Modeling the Spread of an Infectious Disease		
2. Learning objective (from the syllabus): Model the spread of infectious disease using the SIR model in Python.		
3. Specific disciplinary learning objective(s) of the assignment/lab: • Describe the effects of different prevention strategies on the spread of an infectious disease. • Explain how the SIR model can be used to prevent the spread of an infectious disease.		
4. Specific modeling and simulation practice(s): Given a simple model to simulate the spread of infectious disease, students identify the corresponding mathematical model and use computer programming methods to extend an appropriate algorithm representing abstractions of reality via mathematical formulas, constructions, equations, inequalities, constraints, and so forth.		
5. Assessment strategies and grading system: See homework assignment. This will be analyzed using the rubric in appendix D.		
6. Guidance materials and resources such as laboratory manuals and project templates: • Problem description (from this learning design) • Sample Jupyter Notebook, including a simplified version of this model		
7. Instrumentation and software tools: Jupyter Notebooks—Python		
8. Specific instructional events: *A. Teaching method* The instructor will model the start of the lesson by demonstrating how to start the simulation on a Jupyter Notebook. The instructor will then provide scaffolding as discussed in the section "Theoretical Grounding of the Learning Design" with a pre-developed model in a Jupyter Notebook. Students will first *use* this model by explaining to each other how it works. They will then engage in *modifying* the example, using the same Notebook to complete the model as described in the homework assignment. Finally, students will individually complete the homework assignments. *B. Sequencing of activities* • The instructor will present an introduction to the SIR model and will provide the handout that introduces the model to the students. The students will explore the handout and will discuss it in groups to raise any questions before getting into the code. • Next, the instructor will model the work with the Jupyter Notebook and will show the sample Notebook containing a simplified version of the model (see appendix D). The students will work in dyads to explore the Notebook, explain it to each other, and start working together on completing the simulation according to the homework assignment. • The students will then work individually on the homework assignment, which includes the reflection on disciplinary concepts of the spread of an infectious disease.		

Continued

TABLE 3.6 *Continued*

C. Sociology   The students will work in dyads to explore the sample Jupyter Notebook and explain to each other how it works. They will complete the homework individually.
9. Homework (if appropriate):   For this activity, we will simulate the SIR model for a 365-day period and a one million population. The disease we will model has an average recovery time of 15 days and a transmission rate of 15%.   We will simulate three different values for interaction rate and recovery/mortality rates so that we can identify their effect on the number of infected people and on the number of deaths. The following values are suggested as a starting point to run the simulation, but you should propose at least two additional values for each rate: • Contact rate: 2.5   • Recovery rate: 95%   • Mortality rate: 5%   In the end, you should present the following indicators and discuss the implications of (1) having a higher or lower contact rate (e.g., with or without confinement) and (2) increasing or decreasing the recovery rate (e.g., finding new treatments or having limited resources to treat those who are infected):   • Total number of people who got infected   • Total number of people who recovered   • Total number of unaffected people   • Total number of deaths   • Max number of people infected on a given date   • Max number of infections in one day   • Max number of recovered people in one day   • Max number of deaths in one day

Reflection and Lessons Learned

Students, just like everyone living through the COVID pandemic that started in 2020, experienced an uncommon sanitary emergency that had a huge impact on the way we live. Schools and universities closed and moved into an online education modality without enough time to prepare for it. The students needed to stay at home and be aware of not getting their relatives or themselves infected by COVID-19 as well as become skilled at new ways of communicating, interacting, and learning. Over the first few months, the common message in the media was "We need to flatten the curve," emphasizing the value of confinement, masks, and handwashing. However, nobody explained where that curve came from or how we may have a direct impact on the flattening process.

This lesson plan provides an authentic learning experience for 10th graders to learn to program while identifying the value of computing for any subject, including understanding how disease spreads. The lesson plan was piloted with freshmen engineering college students enrolled in an introduction to programming course. Most of the students successfully completed the challenge and highlighted the value of having such a relevant project for something they were experiencing in real life. The lesson plan presented in this learning design provided additional scaffolding (the Jupyter Notebook) for the high school students to be able to engage in the activity, reducing their cognitive load and allowing them to focus on understanding and using the simulation.

Conclusion

This learning design described the lesson plan Modeling the Spread of an Infectious Disease following the cognitive apprenticeship model. The lesson plan engages 10th graders in an authentic task to model the spread of infectious diseases such as COVID-19. The model represents the effects of different measures that we all were exposed to during the pandemic, such as confinement (i.e., reducing the contact rate) and emergent treatments and vaccines (i.e., affecting the recovery rate and the infection rate), with the common goal of "flattening the curve" of infections and deaths.

4

CHAPTER 4 ELABORATES ON THE THEORETICAL FOUNDATIONS USED TO HELP STU-
dents develop computing adaptive expertise and the supports that have resulted in a
pedagogical model called computational cognitive apprenticeship. In addition, the chapter discusses the implications for discipline-based education research—that is, a methodological approach for performing education research in the classroom—along with
opportunities for future work.

TOWARD ADAPTIVE EXPERTISE IN COMPUTATION

Hatano and Inagaki (1986) introduced the concept of adaptive expertise in their work
with Japanese school children. Hatano and Inagaki described the process of how students learn and grow by following two courses of expertise: routine and adaptive. Routine
expertise is often defined by procedural knowledge (i.e., practical knowledge; knowing
how), in which an individual develops efficient skills in a task through long-term repetition and practice. Adaptive expertise is generally characterized by conceptual knowledge (i.e., understanding principles and relationships; knowing why) and the ability to
learn skills in a way that allows them to be transferred between contexts (Bransford,
Brown, and Cocking 2000); in other words, adaptive experts have the ability to quickly
become accustomed to changes in their discipline or work requirements (Hatano and
Inagaki 1986). Adaptive and routine expertise are often depicted as two splitting "paths,"
with routine expertise focused on refining procedural knowledge and adaptive expertise focused on acquiring transferable conceptual knowledge (Bransford, Brown, and
Cocking 2000). This idea of balancing knowledge and skills is further elaborated upon
by Schwartz, Bransford, and Sears (2005) in their two-dimensional model of adaptive
expertise. This model conceptualizes adaptive expertise as a balance of *innovation* and
efficiency, as shown in figure 4.1.

Efficiency is the ability to "rapidly retrieve and accurately apply appropriate knowledge and skills to solve a problem or understand an explanation" (Schwartz, Bransford,
and Sears 2005, 28). Innovation, on the other hand, is the ability to create new solutions
to problems by altering, modifying, or building upon existing knowledge (and sometimes
even creating new knowledge in the process). Innovation involves recognizing and cre-
atively departing from routine approaches, applying multiple strategies to solve novel

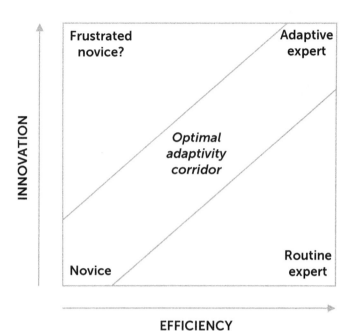

FIGURE 4.1 The development of adaptive expertise through both innovation and efficiency. (Adapted from Schwartz, Bransford, and Sears 2005.)

problems (Schwartz, Bransford, and Sears 2005), and applying strategies for assessing learners' current approaches and attempting to move beyond them (Bransford, Brown, and Cocking 2000). With innovation, individuals need to apply their prior knowledge, identify what they do not know, and utilize their monitoring skills to overcome their difficulties (Hatano and Oura 2003).

Efficiency is important in many domains, particularly in high-production corporations, manufacturing companies, and in many medical positions, such as specialized surgeon. However, a strong focus on developing efficiency often comes at a cost to innovation, as strategies and skills become more familiar and more narrowly applicable to common problems. Likewise, an overfocus on innovation can negatively impact efficiency. Lack of design constraints and too much time spent on any problem may lead to frustration and/or avoidable financial risks during a project. Schwartz, Bransford, and Sears (2005) proposed a new method of thinking about the efficiency–innovation balance by proposing an "optimal adaptability corridor" that learners should be assisted in navigating during university or other training programs. Curricula designed with this adaptability corridor in mind would give students ample time to participate in activities that allow them to work on both sharpening their routine efficiency and flexing their adaptive innovation skills and strategies, with the goal of producing more prepared adaptive experts who are ready to transfer their knowledge into the workforce. With this in mind, three sets of expertise trajectories can be applied to the innovation vs. efficiency model, as shown in figure 4.2.

Trajectory A represents a situation in which too much focus is placed on efficiency and procedural knowledge. This trajectory tends to send students out of the optimal adaptivity corridor and produce routine experts. Although routine expertise is useful in many fields and is the cornerstone of adaptive expertise, it also risks producing a form of cognitive entrenchment in the learner (Dane 2010). Cognitive entrenchment involves viewing currently effective knowledge and methods as the "best" methods, and

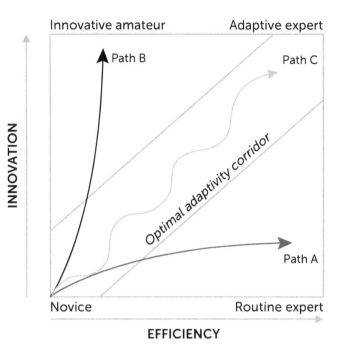

Innovative amateur   Adaptive expert

INNOVATION

Path B

Path C

Optimal adaptivity corridor

Path A

Novice   Routine expert

EFFICIENCY

FIGURE 4.2 Three trajectories within the expertise model.

adopting new approaches becomes difficult. Trajectory B represents a situation where too much focus is placed on innovation and self-directed learning. This trajectory is similar to trajectory A in that it sends students out of the optimal adaptivity corridor, but in the opposite direction, resulting in what we refer to here as an "innovative amateur." These learners are able to devise creative conceptual solutions to new problems but ultimately struggle to implement those solutions effectively due to a lack of procedural expertise. Trajectory C can be considered a more efficient trajectory, where innovation and self-directed learning are balanced by expert guidance (or instructor support) with regard to efficient strategies and the use of procedural knowledge. The goal is for students to develop a more flexible approach to problem-solving and to understand the need to consider novel methods when highly practiced rules and principles do not apply. Therefore, a program focused on the development of adaptive expertise should provide a combination of innovation-oriented and efficiency-oriented constructivist learning activities in order to keep students aligned with trajectory C. How to do this can be a complicated and involved process, as the methods by which learners acquire expertise are still under investigation (Chi 2011).

In our own previous work, we qualitatively characterized the efficiency and innovation dimensions of first-year engineering students' approaches to solving computational modeling and simulation challenges. In our study (Magana et al. 2019), cognitive knowledge, referring to knowledge comprehension, application, analysis, and synthesis, was considered the efficiency dimension of adaptive expertise. Metacognitive knowledge refers to knowledge about the application of strategies and the when, how, and why to apply them, which was considered the innovation dimension of adaptive expertise. Our findings identified four categories; two for the efficiency dimension and two for the innovation dimension. Briefly, in the efficiency dimension, the two main approaches students followed were *implementation-oriented* and *knowledge-oriented*.

While *implementation-oriented* students tended to focus on making their code work, the *knowledge-oriented* students tried to focus on understanding and connecting the disciplinary knowledge with their computing knowledge. Regarding the innovation dimension, the two main approaches students followed were *action-oriented* and *plan-oriented*. While *action-oriented* students tended to jump right into a solution with little or no planning, *plan-oriented* students tended to spend significant time planning their approach before starting to code their solution.

Once we identified each of the four categories (i.e., orientations), we then further inspected how students' experiences and performances related to these categories to uncover the interplay between those four. Two clear and distinct patterns of students' behaviors were noted. Students who exhibited action-oriented and implementation-oriented behaviors were more aligned with novice approaches to expertise. On the other hand, students who exhibited plan-oriented and knowledge-oriented behaviors were more aligned with adaptive expertise. Informed by the work from Riel (2023), we used our findings and mapped them to the different dimensions of adaptive expertise and defined a preliminary characterization of different approaches to expertise in computational modeling and simulation. Table 4.2 in the next section provides descriptions for the four quadrants of the adaptive expertise model that map to each of the corners of figure 4.2. While novices focus on completion, innovative amateurs focus on invention. And while routine experts focus on automaticity, adaptive experts focus on understanding. In the case of adaptive expertise in computation, modeling, and simulation, that understanding takes the form of model-based reasoning (see chapter 2). Table 4.1 elaborates on the four quadrants of the adaptive expertise model, providing descriptions adapted to the context of modeling and simulation.

The question is, How can we support students in their learning and attainment of modeling and simulation practices so they develop adaptive expertise in computation? Based on our previous research, we propose a computational cognitive apprenticeship.

COGNITIVE APPRENTICESHIP MODELS

This section describes the theoretical foundation of a proposed computational cognitive apprenticeship. Informed by more than 15 years of education research in the teaching of computation at the undergraduate level, we have adapted the cognitive apprenticeship model from Collins et al. (1989) to support the teaching and learning of computation in science and engineering education (Fennell et al. 2020; Sanchez-Peña, Vieira, Magana 2022). Apprenticeship models have been used to teach knowledge and skills to train novices to become expert practitioners since the beginning of written history. In many skilled trades, the apprenticeship model is still used to great effect to train individuals in the knowledge and skills needed for a trade or profession. The apprenticeship models employed by many trades and other skill-based professions are, in many ways, inherently situated in their practical context. Apprentices learn in context by observing their instructors as they engage in the practice and taking in the key features of what expert practice "looks like" in that field. The apprentices then hone their skills through

TABLE 4.1 *Operationalization of types of computational expertise*

Novice: Focus on completion
Emphasis on basic performance of the task. Generally unskilled practice with a focus on fulfilling assignment requirements before understanding the content. Low confidence in their practice with a high emphasis on broad, sometimes directionless trial and error until requirements are met. Often results in unsuccessful or inefficient approaches, despite the effort. Focus is placed on producing adequate results and completing assignments for the grade rather than on understanding the content.
Innovative amateur: Focus on invention
Emphasis on making the code run. Highly creative practice with a strong emphasis on trial and error using new practices or procedures. While often successful in generating executable code, there is often little understanding of what factors caused success, and the next effort might be less successful. Willing to try new things and apply a variety of methods to solve the problem, but may lack understanding of why those methods worked, as well as whether or not those methods are the most efficient or appropriate options.
Routine expert: Focus on automaticity
Emphasis on the computational solution. Follows familiar routines or best practices that have been identified as what works, with a strong emphasis on debugging, the efficiency of code, and getting the correct or expected answer. This style of expertise focuses on reducing the time and effort required to produce a computational solution or result. While this form of expertise works well in familiar settings, it is often not well suited to ill-structured problems or problems requiring significant variations to known solution methods. Often focuses on the procedural understanding of how the solution produces results rather than on what those results mean to the solution and/or overall problem.
Adaptive expert: Focus on understanding
Emphasis on combining knowledge and skills. Highly able to connect disciplinary knowledge with computational problem-solving by engaging in computational practices. This form of expertise seeks balance between new and tested methods by allowing the flexibility to generate innovative solutions to problems while still identifying and incorporating elements of known solutions where that will increase efficiency. Adaptive expertise views knowledge as contextual, evolving, and requiring continual adjustment. Therefore, it relies upon and seeks a deeper understanding of the interactions between content knowledge and computational skill. Focuses both on the procedural understanding of the solution and on how results impact the interpretation of the solution, as well as future applications of the method.

Source: Adapted from Riel (2023) and Magana et al. (2019).

a process of "legitimate peripheral participation" (Lave and Wenger 1991) by situating themselves and understanding the practice first, then gradually become more experienced by participating in applying their knowledge to practice in real-world contexts. These activities are often guided and/or monitored by the instructor or are structured in a way that reduces or removes the risk of professional practice (i.e., peripheral), but the learner is nevertheless participating in a "real" (i.e., legitimate) component of the trade or discipline while engaged with peers and superiors within their community of practice.

Apprenticeships are often used in trades and other industries of skilled labor. In contrast, cognitive apprenticeships focus on the didactic methods traditionally used in academic disciplines such as biology or engineering. As discussed in chapter 2, these fields are often taught as a series of courses delivering a body of required background knowledge and testing students through the use of hypothetical or highly abstract pen-and-paper assessments. While pen-and-paper exams are still an effective method of assessing recall and conceptual application of content knowledge, the pedagogy surrounding these assessments often neglects the development of other important skills, critical thinking lenses, and problem-solving strategies associated with the profession. In other words, traditional "lecture and exam" structures often fail to teach students how to think like a practitioner in their discipline.

Collins et al. (1989) proposed a framework for adapting the apprenticeship method to teaching cognitive skills within modern academic topics. Known simply as cognitive apprenticeship, this framework has since been more formalized into a constructivist pedagogical design tool for teaching complex topics both in STEM fields and in other areas of study. The cognitive apprenticeship framework breaks the design of a given learning environment into four key dimensions: content, method, sequencing, and sociology. Each of these dimensions—as well as their subcomponents—are briefly described in table 4.2.

Due to its historical roots, cognitive apprenticeship has been most influential in the laboratory or professional development contexts. The training and professional development of allied health professionals and students often use principles of cognitive apprenticeship (Lyons et al. 2017). Similarly, cognitive apprenticeship principles are frequently used in the professional development of K–12 teachers (Davis, Parker, and Fogle 2019; Peters-Burton et al. 2015) and faculty (Merritt et al. 2018). Additionally, education researchers have repeatedly used cognitive apprenticeship to understand undergraduate and

TABLE 4.2 *Cognitive apprenticeship components with descriptions*

Component	Description
Content	The actual content, knowledge, and skills intended to be taught during the learner's engagement with the course or curriculum. These are divided into domain knowledge, heuristics, control, and learning strategies.
Method	The pedagogical approach, learning strategies, and teaching methods are used to promote the development of expertise. The methods dimension consists of six components: modeling, coaching, scaffolding, articulation, reflection, and exploration.
Sequencing	How activities are ordered to best support learning. Activities can be ordered according to increasing complexity, increasing diversity, and shifting from global to local skills.
Sociology	The social characteristics of the learning environment. This includes teaching through situated learning, establishing a community of practice, promoting a community of practice, and taking advantage of cooperation.

Source: Collins, Brown, and Holum (1991).

graduate research training experiences (Feldon, Shukla, and Maher 2016; Gilmore et al. 2015). The use of cognitive apprenticeship as an instructional approach in classroom settings has been more limited. Among the few available examples are cognitive apprenticeship–based instruction interventions in chemistry and physics (Amalia et al. 2018).

A COMPUTATIONAL COGNITIVE APPRENTICESHIP

With this apprenticeship framework in mind, we can begin to lay out our case for a new cognitive apprenticeship intended to build adaptive expertise in computation, modeling, and simulation. As elaborated in chapter 2 of this book, many of the principles discussed in the cognitive apprenticeship framework can clearly be applied when teaching programming and other computational skills, such as data science (Sanchez-Peña, Vieira, and Magana 2022). However, the acquisition of computational adaptive expertise within the STEM disciplines in which they are now needed is a unique challenge that can be aided by the use of a new type of computation-oriented cognitive apprenticeship: a computational cognitive apprenticeship. The computational cognitive apprenticeship framework stems partly from recent research on incorporating computational methods into undergraduate science and engineering courses using the cognitive apprenticeship approach (Fennell et al. 2020). Such efforts have introduced students to meaningful computational practices through a series of large-scale, discipline-situated programming projects. Here, we describe the unique aspects of applying cognitive apprenticeship to the computational realm and the supporting evidence derived from research.

Content

Design principle: Combine disciplinary domain knowledge with computation, modeling, and simulation practices, techniques, and tools (Fennell et al. 2019; Magana, Ortega-Alvarez, et al. 2017; Ortega-Alvarez, Sanchez, and Magana 2018; Vieira et al. 2018).

This principle can be achieved by utilizing anchored instruction (CTGV 1990), consisting of contextualizing the learning experiences within authentic tasks. Such authentic tasks should occur in real-life contexts and establish meaningful associations between learning experiences and the knowledge, skills, and practices of a discipline (Choi and Hannafin 1995; Magana et al. 2016).

Traditionally, courses designed to teach computational thinking practices, typically within departments of computer science, have a strong focus on programming concepts, principles, and procedures (Tew and Guzdial 2010). Many introductory computing courses that have been developed within engineering disciplines continue to teach much of this basic programming knowledge but expand the scope of their courses to include additional topics (e.g., Narayanan 2007; Stickel 2011). Many courses include computing applications in specific contexts, such as data visualization, data analysis techniques like linear regression, solutions of linear equations, and methods of solution of differential and partial differential equations (Morris et al. 1996). In other courses, the focus expands further to include linking mathematical modeling practices to algorithmic representations in the form of simulations (Magana, Falk, and Reese 2013). A few even touch on tool building in the form of the development of graphical user interfaces.

While expanding the range of computational learning objectives is imperative for STEM disciplines, this expansion runs significant risks. The most obvious risk is the limitation posed by time constraints. Introducing additional disciplinarily focused learning objectives may cause the abandonment of others that are critical to the development of computational thinking (Magana and Coutinho 2017). Furthermore, literature in computer science education has identified for a long time that learning to program is difficult (Lister et al. 2004; McCracken et al. 2001; Soloway and Spohrer 1989). Some of the difficulties learners experience include identifying (1) the purpose of the programming task; (2) the general properties or functionality of the machine that one intends to control; (3) the syntax and semantics of the programming language; (4) structure, where the learner needs to deal with the difficulties of acquiring standard patterns or schemas that can be implemented to attain small-scale goals; and (5) pragmatics, where the learner develops the skills to be able to specify, develop, test, and debug programs using whatever tools are available (Du Boulay 1986; Pea and Kurland 1983).

Our prior research also indicates that in addition to programming challenges, certain practices, particularly those that demand the integration of differing representations (i.e., physical, mathematical, and algorithmic such as occur in modeling and simulation), run significant risks of causing cognitive overload (Magana, Falk, and Reese, 2013; Vieira, Roy, et al. 2016). Cognitive load happens when short-term memory is insufficient to successfully undertake complex processes that interrelate multiple novel concepts. During our research performed in classroom settings, we have identified that programming preparation grounded in anchored instruction provided an important foundation beyond increasing students' control self-beliefs (i.e., one's appraisals of control over achievement activities and outcomes). This preparation seemed to effectively enable students to leverage computational practices for the purpose of acquiring disciplinary concepts (Magana et al. 2016). That is, although the students generally came into the course with a limited, novice-like ability to engage with computational tools and procedures, research on the outcomes of the course over multiple semesters showed that more intensive exposure to modeling and simulation methods tended to improve students' self-efficacy beliefs about their ability to use computational tools and interpret simulation data (Magana, Falk, and Reese 2013; Magana et al. 2016).

Method

Design principle: Provide scaffolding to students in the form of code snippets, test cases, and worked-out examples (Vieira et al. 2019; Vieira, Roy, et al. 2016; Vieira, Yan, and Magana 2015), and consider providing students agency to select the scaffolding they need (Vieira et al. 2020), or fade the scaffolding progressively (Fennell et al. 2019; Vieira et al. 2017; Vieira et al. 2019).

The method dimension is particularly broad in the context of computing education. In our own prior work (Magana, Falk, and Reese 2013), we considered a course developed using the How People Learn (HPL) framework (Bransford, Brown, and Cocking 2000) that emphasized, among other dimensions, knowledge-centered and learner-centered instructional practices. In that course, a sequence was adopted in which in-class exercises would proceed from students being presented with a working code to read and execute. Next, students were provided with a code, but that code was either malfunctioning, incomplete, or required an extension. The final exercise involved developing a code to meet a specification that was at least conceptually related to the first two codes. The course was observed to result in high student self-assessments of knowledge of programming, the utility of computation, and intention to continue pursuing computing opportunities in their studies and careers.

Based on our initial explorations of how we could provide instructional support to students, we then formalized a worked-out example approach that was deployed and evaluated as a means to mitigate the issue of cognitive overload discussed in the prior section (Vieira, Roy, et al. 2016, Vieira, Yan, and Magana 2015). In the most successful deployment, students were provided with access to step-by-step examples of sample solutions to programming problems. These solutions included conceptualization of the problem, algorithm development, and programming, resulting in a final working but uncommented code. In our work, we identified that a very effective strategy to engage students in understanding worked-out examples was having them write in-code comments (Vieira et al. 2017). Students were required to comment on this code for the first four such examples as a strategy to self-explain them. These were graded. Subsequently, worked-out examples could be commented on for extra credit. Students reported such practices to be useful for their learning.

Sequencing

Design principle: Enact the problem-solving process as steps for guiding the modeling and simulation process (Fennell et al. 2017; Shaikh et al. 2015; Vieira, Magana, et al. 2016).

Sequencing plays a key role in structuring student learning by providing experiences that support the acquisition of knowledge and its deployment by embedding it within clear and, in some instances, familiar contexts and then gradually removing these contextual supports. In this way, sequencing can provide stepping stones toward increasing adaptive expertise by encouraging students to deploy their new knowledge in successively less structured and more unfamiliar contexts. For instance, scaffolding at a course level has been used as an approach in which current student learning of computation content is anchored or bridged by a generalization of what the student has already assimilated from previous learning (Sticklen et al. 2004). Specifically, the course in question built on familiar concepts by beginning with scalar operations and then moving to vector and array operations (Sticklen et al. 2004).

Another scaffolding technique is the use-modify-create approach (Malyn-Smith and Lee 2012; NRC 2011), which has been identified as a potential strategy to introduce computational practices to novice learners. These three phases guide students to a process where they first inspect the code (use), then transition to changing the code to fit an intended action (modify), and finally generate a new model (create), having ownership over its development (Lee et al. 2011). In a comparative study, Lytle et al. (2019) identified that the use-modify-create sequence provided students a natural learning evolution while giving them more ownership over the artifacts they created.

A different sequencing strategy was deployed in our own design-based research to help students structure their work on complex projects (Vieira, Roy, et al. 2016). During the initial problem recognition phase, the student works to understand the problem and create a plan to work toward a solution. The student uses verbal and mathematical representations for this purpose. In the second phase, called problem framing, the student executes the plan to create a solution in the form of an algorithm instantiated as a program. Finally, in the problem synthesis phase, the student completes the plan by evaluating the solution according to both instructor-provided and student-generated criteria. The implementation of test cases is one of the most challenging phases for students and one of the most valuable for those who go on to programming practice in any context (Vieira et al. 2015).

Sociology

Design principle: Implement pedagogical approaches that promote collaboration within a context or culture of disciplinary practices (Lyon and Magana 2021).

This design principle goes hand in hand with the content principle, as sociology also emphasizes learning within the context of realistic tasks (CTGV 1990). Previous work that focuses on integrating the sociology component has primarily described the way programming content has been combined with engineering problem-solving (e.g., Azemi and Pauley 2006; Devens 1999; Hrynuk et al. 2008; Luchini, Colbry, and Punch 2007; Morrell 2007; Morris et al. 1996). However, the sociology component is one of the least explored aspects of integrating computation in engineering education. As part of the content principle, we have elaborated on how we utilized anchored instruction as a sociology approach for integrating computation within disciplinary engineering practices (Magana et al. 2016). But more research is needed on how to properly orchestrate the sociology of learning inside and outside of the classroom.

In our classroom implementations, we have deployed a flipped-classroom design to free up class time for more hands-on and group learning activities, which were monitored closely during class by the instructor and the TAs. This gave students extended periods of time (in and out of class) to complete each project, allowing plenty of time for students to seek help from the instructional staff when they get stuck and for them to work together with their peers throughout the problem-solving process.

Another well-known approach in computer science and electrical and computer engineering that can effectively integrate the sociology aspect into programming assignments is pair programming (Braught, Wahls, and Eby 2011; Fila and Loui 2014). This approach is usually implemented in dyads where two students work on the same computer. One of the students takes the role of the driver and has the keyboard control to perform the programming, while the other takes the copilot role. The copilot thinks about the problem and shares some ideas without touching the keyboard. Students may alternate roles from time to time, usually every 5 to 10 minutes. This strategy would be worth exploring in engineering education.

In our most recent work implementing modeling and simulation challenges within the context of a capstone course, we saw success in having students work within teams as they planned and evaluated their modeling solutions (Arigye, Udosen, et al. 2023; Lyon and Magana 2021). Having students work in teams or groups as they plan their modeling solution allows individuals to exchange different ideas and ways of solving a problem, something that is beneficial for students as they explore a new modeling problem (Diefes-Dux, Hjalmarson, and Zawojewski 2013). Allowing students to compare their solutions with other students and teams as they evaluate their models enables them to see multiple ways of solving a problem. This experience gives students the opportunity to see how certain modeling solutions are better or worse, as well as different limitations and assumptions that can be made during the problem-solving process. Seeing multiple ways of solving a modeling problem can aid students in future problem-solving endeavors (Kapur and Bielaczyc 2012).

NEW RESEARCH DIRECTIONS

Computational cognitive apprenticeship brings an understanding of the learning environment of the higher education classroom into the fold, adding much-needed pedagogical and sociological considerations to the study of computation in the context of STEM domains. This new framework of computational cognitive apprenticeship has implications for and leads to new research directions in discipline-based education research generally (NASEM 2012) and the computational and data science education space specifically (NASEM 2018). First, specific cases of how to apply computational apprenticeship are needed within higher education contexts, along with a deeper understanding of the impact this framework has in building these skills as students head into the workforce. Design-based research and action research are two methods in which these specific experiences and pedagogies can be investigated within the classroom (Barab and Squire 2004; Brydon-Miller, Greenwood, and Maguire 2003). Specifically, by doing practitioner research through design-based research, researchers can build pedagogy to answer national calls for computational and data science in the context of STEM domains and study the application of and extend theory around the use of computational apprenticeship within the classroom. Figure 4.3 presents the stages of design-based research and the outcomes and contributions derived from its implementation.

Design-based research is similar to engineering design as it starts by identifying a need. As shown in figure 4.3, design-based research starts with a learning need, as elaborated in chapter 1 of this book. We have made a case that students need to develop model-based reasoning to effectively engage in computation, modeling, and simulation practices in STEM. The left side of figure 4.3 depicts stages involved with the design of learning interventions grounded in evidence-based practices, as elaborated in chapter 2 of this book. As researchers and practitioners engage in the design and implementation of learning interventions, new knowledge is created in the form of (1) new pedagogies or scaffolding methods, (2) design knowledge in the form of pedagogical principles, (3) useful artifacts such as computational tools and methods, and (4) exemplars of

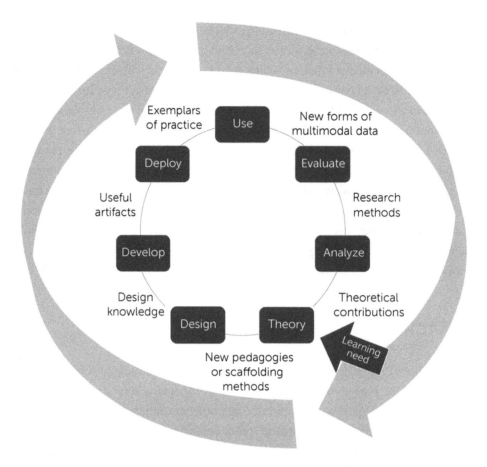

FIGURE 4.3 Stages of design-based research and potential outcomes and contributions from each stage.

practice including how materials and pedagogies are orchestrated and enacted in classroom settings. In addition, design-based research allows researchers and practitioners to develop theoretical contributions as learning interventions are evaluated and investigated in classroom settings. The right side of figure 4.3 depicts the stages involved in researching the effects of learning interventions. As innovations are used in the classroom or other educational settings, data is generated that can further provide insights into how students learn, how students interact with the technology, and artifacts and process data created in the process. To make meaning of this data, new research methods can be developed in the space of educational data mining and learning analytics. As data is analyzed and interpreted under specific conceptual, theoretical, or methodological frameworks, new knowledge can be derived, contributing to findings in discipline-based education research (Magana 2022). As shown in figure 4.3, iterative cycles are performed in order to refine the learning innovation and the theoretical contributions.

Research is also needed to investigate whether principles derived from computational cognitive apprenticeship can be applied to teaching and learning other computational thinking practices and result in computational adaptive expertise. Weintrop et al. (2016) identified a taxonomy for the use and application of computational thinking in the context of science and mathematics. Although originally proposed for K–12 education, this taxonomy can also be adopted and adapted for undergraduate STEM education. Figure 4.4 presents a modified version of the taxonomy. As shown in figure 4.4, the taxonomy considers data practices, computational problem-solving practices, modeling and simulation practices, systems thinking practices, and intelligent machine design practices. Weintrop's taxonomy considers only the first four of these practices (starting at the bottom of figure 4.4). However, due to the relevance of artificial intelligence (AI) in society, learning AI concepts and practices at the K–12 and undergraduate levels has become critical. To take steps toward introducing AI concepts in the curriculum, the Artificial Intelligence for K–12 Initiative (AI4K12 2020) identified five big ideas in AI. These five big ideas are guidelines that serve as a framework to assist curricular developers with AI concepts, essential knowledge, and skills. We have adopted and adapted elements of those ideas, incorporating them at the top of figure 4.4. The guidelines and lessons learned presented in this book have mainly focused on modeling and simulation practices, with elements of computational problem-solving practices. But more classroom-based or naturalistic research is needed to further identify whether the same suggestions, guidelines, and design principles apply to all practices depicted in figure 4.4.

The development of adaptive expertise is dependent on a balance of innovation and efficiency during the learning process. While efficiency in specific skills can be built through rote practice and repetition, the integration of skills required to form

Intelligent machine design practices	• Engineering of intelligent machines and programs (AI) • Creating systems able to learn without being explicitly programmed (ML) • Implementing systems capable of learning based on deep neural networks (DL)
Systems thinking practices	• Investigating systems as a whole • Understanding the relationships/subsystems within a system • Communicating a system's component
Modeling and simulation practices	• Using computational models to characterize phenomena • Constructing computational models • Validating and verifying computational models
Computational problem-solving practices	• Programming • Creating computational abstractions • Troubleshooting and debugging
Data practices	• Collecting and creating data • Curating and manipulating data • Analyzing and visualizing data

FIGURE 4.4 A conceptual framework for characterizing computational thinking practices in STEM. (Adapted from Weintrop 2016.)

capabilities occurs when learners are prompted to combine skills in new ways in order to solve unfamiliar or ill-structured problems. The computational cognitive apprenticeship framework is key in facilitating the development of computational adaptive expertise, as it provides a safe, guided environment in which students may engage in computational innovation. This allows for the broadening and combination of individual skills as the learner moves through the apprenticeship toward an adaptive capability for computational modeling and simulation. However, it is also possible that pedagogies with less scaffolding that delay instruction and feedback can be equally effective. Such pedagogies are aligned with productive failure approaches (Kapur 2010; Lyon and Magana 2021; Schwartz et al. 2011). Productive failure approaches provide parameters to guide students to invent solutions before receiving formal instruction (Schwartz et al. 2011). Considering figure 4.2, it is possible that productive failure approaches can be equally effective as cognitive apprenticeship approaches but perhaps promote a learning trajectory as path B (see figure 4.2). We have implemented productive failure approaches in our research, but more in the context of capstone courses (Lyon and Magana 2021, 2019). This design decision was made based on the students' level of disciplinary knowledge. This population of students was in their last semester before graduating; thus, we deemed it feasible to implement a pedagogy with less scaffolding and guidance and more articulation and reflection (Jaiswal et al. 2021). However, more research is needed in this direction to identify the trajectories students may follow toward adaptive expertise and whether there is a variation in the level of innovation or efficiency depending on the pedagogical supports.

Additionally, the understanding of how to fairly measure and assess computational practices will need to continue to develop within research trajectories. One major limitation of empirical studies so far within the literature has been the difficulty of measuring and assessing computational thinking, which is highly interconnected with computational modeling and simulation (Lyon and Magana 2020; Magana and Coutinho 2017). While some taxonomies of computational thinking exist (Malyn-Smith and Lee 2012; Weintrop et al. 2016), as well as computational thinking knowledge tests that focus heavily on programming knowledge (Caceffo et al. 2016; Tang et al. 2020), continued work on assessing these skills is needed to understand the effectiveness of the computational apprenticeship framework.

Longitudinal studies on the effects of implementing computational cognitive apprenticeship pedagogy over the course of multiple years are needed to understand the cumulative effects of these experiences on student outcomes. Forms of curricular models such as spiral curricula are reported as being useful for integrating skills such as computational modeling and simulation into the classroom (Magana and Silva Coutinho 2017). More work is needed to identify the evolution of pedagogical practices as students develop their skills. We have made an argument that productive failure approaches could be more suitable for advanced students, while cognitive apprenticeship approaches could be more suitable for novice learners. However, research is needed to identify the transition from heavily supported scaffolding and fading approaches to removing support (Noroozi et al. 2018). For instance, figure 4.5 proposes a progression for providing support at the beginning of the learning process and gradually removing supports by

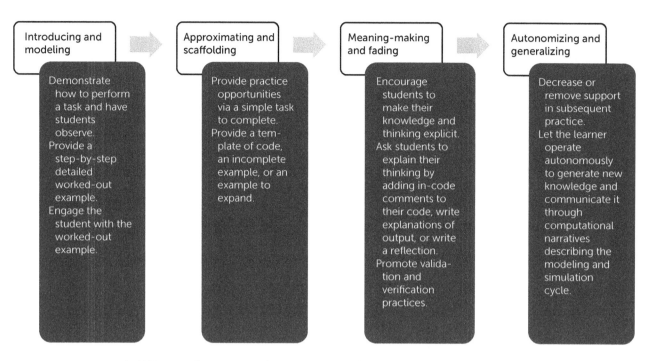

FIGURE 4.5 A progression from increasing to fading scaffolding in computation.

eliciting articulation from students and by providing more autonomy in the learning process. This progression aligns with the instructional strategies proposed by Collins et al. (1991): modeling, coaching, scaffolding, articulation, reflection, and exploration. In the case of the progression proposed in figure 4.5, students are guided by (1) providing worked-out examples that explicitly connect disciplinary concepts with variables and behaviors of the computational model; (2) providing incomplete programming tasks for students to complete a model or to program simple models; (3) eliciting students to make their thinking explicit by writing in-code comments of their code or that of others, and making explicit connections between the disciplinary concepts and the computational solution; and (4) removing all supports, providing students autonomy in creating their own computational solutions, and providing additional practice and opportunities to reflect. This progression needs to be validated through classroom research.

Furthermore, different types of scaffolding methods can be used to better support students in the development of the cognitive and metacognitive skills needed to develop computational adaptive expertise. Specifically, Quintana et al. (2004) proposed a scaffolding framework consisting of four different methods, as shown in figure 4.6:

Sensemaking scaffolding: Helping students relate to and transform different representations.

Articulation scaffolding: Guiding students in integrating their prior knowledge with new knowledge and making this connection explicit.

Process management scaffolding: Providing explicit guidance to enact disciplinary practices and problem-solving strategies used by experts.

Reflection scaffolding: Leading to students improving their skills and processes through personal reflection on their lived experiences.

Sensemaking	Articulation	Process management	Reflection
Supports ways to understand real-world phenomena or experiences and transform those into formal representations.	Supports ways of making thinking explicit, synthesizing explanations, and creating arguments.	Supports the use of disciplinary practices, problem-solving, and strategic approaches.	Supports the reviewing, reflecting on, and evaluating results, including elements of collaboration.

FIGURE 4.6 Scaffolding methods to support cognitive and metacognitive processes.

The pedagogical methods evaluated through research presented in this book (e.g., figure 4.5) have primarily aligned with sensemaking scaffolding (e.g., worked-out examples and code snippets). However, there are articulation scaffolding methods, such as eliciting students' explanations of their thinking in the form of arguments. Arguments are scientific explanations that help students connect claims, evidence, and reasoning. An argumentation framework can be used to guide students and help them connect claims by making predictions before executing a computational model, connect evidence by making explicit observations on the graphs and plots derived from the model execution, and connect reasoning back to disciplinary knowledge (McNeill and Krajcik 2008). Process management scaffolding could include project or laboratory templates that guide students through the problem-based learning cycle, the inquiry cycle, or the modeling and simulation cycle. Many of the stages of these cycles are often assumed. For example, the planning stage is sometimes overlooked by faculty. In chapter 2, we made an argument about the relevance of process and product learning outcomes. With guidance through process stages, students could also develop metacognitive skills required in the enactment of computation, modeling, and simulation practices, such as model validation and verification. Finally, reflection scaffolding could also help reinforce the development of metacognitive knowledge by guiding learners through personal reflection on their learning and learning processes and enacted collaborative learning and team processes. Reflective practices could also elicit students to think about strategies to change in future iterations or implementations. For instance, students could reflect upon strategies to improve troubleshooting or team coordination processes.

Our work has focused on understanding how computational cognitive apprenticeship can be used in a specific class or instructional unit. However, investigation of how computational adaptive expertise develops and plays out over an entire undergraduate curriculum is needed to fully understand the impact of the proposed computational cognitive apprenticeship. The scope should not be limited to undergraduate years, as these highly needed professional skills require studying in professional and continuing education contexts. Thus, there is a need to understand how these skills develop all the way through the undergraduate years and even into graduate coursework and professional years.

Using cognitive apprenticeship within computing courses has also been shown to significantly lower dropout rates (Vihavainen, Paksula, and Luukkainen 2011). The computational apprenticeship framework offers a constructivist perspective on understanding and addressing these issues. For example, several studies have demonstrated that scaffolding computing instruction within authentic problem-solving contexts can support underrepresented groups' interests and academic achievement in computing (Goode and Margolis 2011; Kafai et al. 2014; Yardi and Bruckman 2007). More research is needed to investigate the effectiveness of these methods among students with diverse backgrounds.

In addition, the social coding movement continues to produce platforms such as interactive computational documents or notebooks that permit integrating multimedia resources (e.g., equations, text, visualizations) with code (Klever 2020). Markdown, Azure, Databricks, Google Collaboratory, MATLAB Live, and Jupyter are some of the most widely adopted (Chattopadhyay et al. 2020). Computational documents permit authoring and executing code within a single document launched through a web browser, which can lower initial barriers to programming. This environment is suitable for novice programmers as they can program without dealing with the installation of compilers or integrated development environments (Lucas Lacal 2020). These platforms can facilitate the use of scaffolding approaches such as fill-in-the-blank and use-modify-create (Lee et al. 2011) that integrate sequencing into computational lessons. Additionally, the ability to comment and embed rich text can help to make observable the heuristics and other metacognitive processes employed by experts during computational problem-solving processes. Furthermore, computational documents can provide students with opportunities to share work, keep track of details, and collaborate in the process (Wang et al. 2019), thus enabling the sociology of learning. Because of such affordances, it is not surprising that interactive documents have now been adopted in educational environments (O'Hara, Blank, and Marshall 2015). In our more recent work (i.e., Arigye, Magana, et al. 2023), we have successfully used computational notebooks to deploy all elements of the computational cognitive apprenticeship, where students were guided through sensemaking, articulation, process management, and reflection scaffolding.

CONCLUSION

THE NEED FOR COMPUTATION IS SPREADING ACROSS STEM DISCIPLINES. IN LIGHT of this, computational adaptive experts has never been more necessary within all disciplines and in every industry sector. The pairing of adaptive expertise models with a cognitive apprenticeship within computational disciplines, a framework we have proposed as *computational cognitive apprenticeship*, may be best suited to address this growing challenge. Through the use of authentic disciplinary experiences to advance students from routine experts or frustrated novices to adaptive experts, a computational cognitive apprenticeship can meet the increasing demands for computational thinking–enabled professionals.

The goal of the computational apprenticeship model is to help learners turn the skills acquired during training into broader capabilities in future practice while they are still in training. Teaching through the apprenticeship model helps prepare students to address unfamiliar problems in the field by making the thinking and experience of experts in the discipline visible throughout the learning process. This paves the way for adaptive expertise, as practitioners who are well-prepared to apply computation in the field by thinking like an expert will be better able to address unfamiliar problems as they arise. While a skilled practitioner may be able to address common problems quickly and efficiently, a capable practitioner can apply known skills efficiently and develop new skills as needed. The computational apprenticeship framework builds capability rather than just skills by providing the learner with a discipline-situated environment that reflects the knowledge structures and hands-on experience needed to turn knowledge and skills into flexible capabilities.

The computational cognitive apprenticeship framework helps develop more adaptive expert capabilities by facilitating carefully guided learning of practical and transferable skills. The generalization of specific computational thinking skills into a holistic set of core computational capabilities prepares the learner to address new problems in practice. The computational apprenticeship framework helps students to gradually expand the integration (and therefore usefulness) of their skill sets over time. This enables them to address more and more complex and varied problems, until they are prepared to set off on their own in the workforce or academia.

Many areas need further exploration in order to formalize and operationalize this framework in educational settings. These explorations can be accomplished mainly through the use of design-based and longitudinal research settings. Additionally, knowledge of how to measure and assess computational modeling and simulation practices is required for us to progress in our understanding of how to build the transfer needed to create computational adaptive experts. But once implemented, these authentic learning experiences provide the opportunity to increase the knowledge and abilities of those in the current pipelines of computational fields and increase and broaden the participation of those entering the pipelines to begin with.

APPENDIX A

Sample Project and Solution for Designing for Novice Learners

PROJECT DESCRIPTION

Introduction

> The most common cause of cardiac arrest is a heart rhythm disorder or arrhythmia called ventricular fibrillation (VF). The heart has a built-in electrical system. In a healthy heart, a "pacemaker" triggers the heartbeat, then electrical impulses run along pathways in the heart, causing it to contract in a regular, rhythmic way. When a contraction happens, blood is pumped. But in ventricular fibrillation, the electrical signals that control the pumping of the heart suddenly become rapid and chaotic. As a result, the lower chambers of the heart, the ventricles, begin to quiver (fibrillate) instead of contract, and they can no longer pump blood from the heart to the rest of the body. If blood cannot flow to the brain, it becomes starved of oxygen, and the person loses consciousness in seconds. Unless an emergency shock is delivered to the heart to restore its regular rhythm using a machine called a defibrillator, death can occur within minutes. It's estimated that more than 70% of ventricular fibrillation victims die before reaching the hospital.
>
> —HEART RHYTHM SOCIETY (HTTPS://WWW.HRSONLINE.ORG/)

This week you will be writing a computer program that will simulate the passage of an electrical pulse through the heart muscle. The model we will use is extremely oversimplified (e.g., Ottesen, Olufsen, and Larsen 2006), but it has the ability to model a phenomenon that is suspected to lie at the heart of one of the most common causes of cardiac arrest: ventricular fibrillation. This is the state where the contraction of the muscle becomes disorganized and is no longer able to adequately pump blood. This condition is familiar to anyone who watches medical dramas on television. When this happens on *Gray's Anatomy* or *ER*, someone grabs "the cart," yells "Clear!" and gives the person who just passed out a jolt of electricity in an effort to reestablish a normal cardiac rhythm. Unfortunately, in real life, 85% of those who go into ventricular fibrillation will not be able to get help in time to save their life. Devising minimally invasive and effective techniques to reverse ventricular fibrillation is therefore an important medical issue.

Modeling Heart Tissue

We will keep track of two aspects of the heart tissue: the local potential, which we will call U, and the depletion of the tissue, V. We will define V as follows: when it is zero, the tissue is most excitable, and when it increases, the tissue has used up all its local ability to create a potential. While tissue remains at a high potential, it gradually becomes more depleted. But when the tissue is not at high potential, its depletion reduces and it becomes more excitable. To model this, we say that the rate of depletion is proportional to $U - V$. That is to say, the degree of depletion goes up as U goes up, but it will go down if U is less than V.

We can model this process by considering how much the tissue is depleted at time $t + \Delta t$ if we know the depletion in the tissue at time t, and the potential at time t:

$$V(t + \Delta t) = V(t) + \Delta t\ (U(t) - V(t)) = (1 - \Delta t)\ V(\ t\ ) + \Delta t\ U(\ t\ ) \tag{0.1}$$

Here Δt is the step in time we are making at each tick of our clock. For our purposes $\Delta t = 0.0494$. So, if we know U and V at any time, we can predict V at a later time.

The behavior of the potential is more complex. In fact, there are three cases we will consider. To discern these cases, we must define a critical value of U that we will call U^*. U^* is the value of U above which the electrical potential has to get to excite the tissue. U^* depends on the level of depletion in the region of tissue. We define U^* to be

$$U^*(t) = (V(t) + 0.01)\ /\ 0.3 \tag{0.2}$$

Case 1: U < 0.0001

In this case, the system is unexcited, and we can just assume $U = 0$ and will stay 0.

Note in this case

$$U_{excite}(t + \Delta t) = 0 \tag{1.1}$$

$$V(t + \Delta t) = (1 - \Delta t)\ V(t) \tag{1.2}$$

Case 2: 0.0001 < U < U*

In this case, the system is not yet above the excitement threshold. In this case

$$U_{excite}(t + \Delta t) = \frac{U(t)}{1 - 10{,}000\Delta t[1 - U(t)][U(t) - U^*(t)]} \tag{2.1}$$

$$V(t + \Delta t) = (1 - \Delta t)\ V(t) + \Delta t\ U(t) \tag{2.2}$$

Case 3: U > U*

In this case, the tissue has been excited

$$U_{excite}(t + \Delta t) = \frac{U(t)\{1 + 10{,}000\Delta t[U(t) - U^*(t)]\}}{1 + 10{,}000\Delta t\, U(t)[U(t) - U^*(t)]} \qquad (3.1)$$

$$V(t + \Delta t) = (1 - \Delta t)\, V(t) + \Delta t\, U(t) \qquad (3.2)$$

Diffusion of the Electrical Potential

When the electrical potential is excited, it doesn't stay in one place. It spreads out. As a result, the potential tends to even out over time. Areas of particularly high potential tend to decrease. Areas of low potential next to regions of high potential increase. This process is called diffusion.

Consider the concentration as being defined on a square grid with rows r and columns c (as shown in figure A.1). To figure out if the potential in a location (r,c) goes up or down, we have to compare it to the average concentration in the neighboring boxes. The way we can simulate this numerically is to define the average concentration in the boxes adjacent to (r,c) at time t to be

$$U_{AVG}(r, c, t) = [U(r - 1, c, t) + U(r + 1, c, t) + U(r, c - 1, t) + U(r, c + 1, t)]\,/\,4 \qquad (4.1)$$

Then the change in U at time t would be

$$U(r, c, t + \Delta t) = U_{excite}(r, c, t + \Delta t) + \Delta t\, D\,(U_{AVG}(r, c, t) - U(r, c, t)) \qquad (4.2)$$

So, if the average potential in the surrounding boxes is higher than U, then $U_{AVG} > U$ and U will increase. If the surrounding boxes are, on average, lower in potential than U, then U will decrease. D gives the rate at which this process occurs. We will use a value of D = 4.1. Note that this change is in addition to and simultaneous with any changes to U from equations 1.1, 2.1, or 3.1 above. So, for example, when simulating a cell that fits Case 2, you would then have

$$U(r, c, t + \Delta t) = \frac{U(r, c, t)}{1 - 10{,}000[1 - U(r, c, t)][U(r, c, t) - U^*(r, c, t)]} + \Delta t\, D\,[U_{AVG}(r, c, t) - U(r, c, t)] \qquad (4.3)$$

The other consideration we must worry about is what happens along the edge of our piece of heart tissue. Since there are no neighboring boxes along the edge, the above procedure is not well-defined for boxes along the boundary. What you will do is compute the new concentrations everywhere on the grid and then set the edge boxes to be equal in concentration to the neighboring boxes just inside the edge (as shown in figure A.2). This ensures that the profiles are flat at the boundary.

1	2	3	4	5	6	7	8
9	10	11	12	13	14	15	16
17	18	19	20	21	22	23	24
25	26	27	28	29	30	31	32
33	34	35	36	37	38	39	40
41	42	43	44	45	46	47	48
49	50	51	52	53	54	55	56
57	58	59	60	61	62	63	64

FIGURE A.1 An 8 × 8 matrix labeled sequentially row by row, illustrating the initial data in the 64 cells.

10	10	11	12	13	14	15	15
10	10	11	12	13	14	15	15
18	18	19	20	21	22	23	23
26	26	27	28	29	30	31	31
34	34	35	36	37	38	39	39
42	42	43	44	45	46	47	47
50	50	51	52	53	54	55	55
50	50	51	52	53	54	55	55

FIGURE A.2 The same matrix as shown in figure A.1, but where the data in the outermost rows and columns has been replaced by the data in the next-innermost cell to impose an outgoing-wave boundary condition.

The diagrams in figures A.1 and A.2 represent the originally calculated concentration. The black squares are not calculated properly because they have no neighbors. In the grid to the right, they are replaced by the values from neighboring cells.

Code Structure

Write a program that will simulate the above process. It should contain the following procedures:

```
function U = StimTissue(U, r, c)
% Takes an N × N array and stimulates a circular region with radius N / 8
% centered at row r and column c by setting the values of U in that
% region to 0.8.
```

function [U, V] = InitTissue(N)
% This function will create an initial condition where U and V are
% N × N arrays that are zero everywhere except for a circle of radius
% N / 8 centered at row (N + 1) / 2 and col (N + 1) / 2, which should have U = 0.8.
% Use the StimTissue procedure defined above.

function [newU, newV] = StepTissue(U, V, D, dt)
% This procedure will advance the clock on U and V by one time step.

function SimTissue(N, T, stime, ptime, D, dt)
% Simulates a tissue that is represented by two N × N arrays. The
% simulation lasts T time steps. It is initially set up with a
% stimulus at the center using InitTissue. Every stime steps a randomly
% located region of radius N / 8 is electrically stimulated. The values
% in U should be plotted as a pcolor plot every ptime steps.

function TestTissue(N, T, stime, r, c, ptime, D, dt)
% Simulates a tissue that is represented by two N × N arrays. The
% simulation lasts T time steps. It is initially set up with a
% stimulus at the center using InitTissue. Once, after stime steps,
% a region centered on row r and column c of radius N / 8 is
% stimulated. The values in U should be plotted as a pcolor plot
% every ptime steps.

Hints

1. There is a built-in function called **del2** that may be helpful.
2. It is important to note that once a pcolor plot happens in an axis, any button click will be captured by the surface object returned by the pcolor plot, not by the axis.

Part I: Planning

You are required to plan your approach to this project and submit this plan by Friday at 6:00 p.m. To give you an idea of what we are looking for, an example plan for a generic coding problem is provided on the Blackboard website. The purpose of submitting your plan is for you to take the time to think through the different parts of the project so that you have a roadmap for your work. Note that there are four parts of the work that should be addressed in your plan:

Designing: What is the design for the solution? What are the critical parts of the problem? What are the inputs and outputs? If there is graphical output, what will this output look like? How will parts of your solution utilize or connect to other parts?

Coding: What control structures, iteration techniques, built-in functions, or other programming techniques will you need to use? Diagram flow charts of some of your subroutines.

Testing: What are some example cases you would want to test to make sure the subroutines work along the way? What are some example cases you could think of to test the final program?

Debugging: How will you check for bugs, particularly those that do not result in syntax errors? Are there parts that you anticipate will create problems due to their complexity? Could these be broken down into simpler pieces that could be debugged separately?

Make sure your pan references the project description and identifies the most relevant aspects of the project. Your plan will be judged according to how well thought out it is. We will try to provide feedback on this plan by Sunday.

To communicate your plan, feel free to use regular paper, a whiteboard, sticky notes, or any medium of choice. Submit these by saving them as pdfs using a scanner or an app like iScanner, Turbo Scan, Tiny Scan for iPhone, or similar to produce a good quality and reasonably sized single pdf file that you can submit via Blackboard. You may work in a team on this plan as long as you include all team members' names on the submission. All other parts of the assignment must be done on your own.

Part II: Coding and Testing

The programming part of your assignment should be contained in five files called **StimTissue.m, InitTissue.m, StepTissue.m, SimTissue.m,** and **TestTissue.m**. In addition, you should submit a pdf that shows the results from running your code on the provided test cases and three additional test cases of your own design. Make sure to document why you chose these test cases and what output you expect.

Part III: Application

Once you have completed your coding and testing, use your code to answer the following questions in a separate pdf file. Include at least two images that illustrate your points. To explore these, make sure your simulation size is at least N = 160. You will need to simulate times of approximately 100 steps or more to make adequate observations.

1. What happens when you stimulate the tissue only once at the beginning and not at subsequent times? Describe. Would this represent normal or abnormal heart function? (5 points)

2. Under what conditions do self-sustaining excitations occur in the cardiac tissue? What do these look like? Describe a controlled numerical experiment with only two stimulations of the tissue that can trigger this abnormal behavior. Give the timing and the location of the second stimulation with respect to the first.

PROJECT SOLUTION

I. Solution for the Modeling of Heart Tissue

```
function U = StimTissue(U, r, c)
%% this procedure will stimulate the field U at a location (r,c) in a
%% circular region of radius N/8
     N = length(U);                          %% find N
     [cols, rows] = meshgrid(1:N,1:N);   %% specify stimulated region
     where = (rows-r).^2+(cols-c).^2 < (N/8)^2;
     U(where)=0.8;                           %% set stimulated region
end

function [U, V] = InitTissue(N)
%% this procedure will initialize two N × N matrices called U and V
%% V will be zeroed everywhere
%% U will have a stimulated region in the center
     U=zeros(N);
     V=zeros(N);
     U=StimTissue(U,(N+1)/2,(N+1)/2);
end

function [newU, newV] = StepTissue(U, V, D, dt)
%% this procedure will advance the clock on U and V by one time step
     newU=U;     %% initialize matrices for the values at the future time
     newV=V;     %% compute a value used to discriminate different regions
     UminusUstar = U - ( V + 0.01 ) / 0.3;
     %% calculate logical masks for regions depending on U value
     case1 = U<0.0001;
     case2 = UminusUstar<0;
     %% calculate the new U value differently depending on the region
     newU(case1)=0;
     newU(~case1 & case2) = U(~case1 & case2)./...
          (1-10000*dt.*(1-U(~case1 & case2)).*UminusUstar(~case1 &
     case2));
     newU(~case2) = U(~case2).*(1+10000*dt.*UminusUstar(~case2))./...
          (1+10000*dt.*U(~case2).*UminusUstar(~case2));
     %% include the effect of diffusion
     newU = newU + D*dt*del2(U);
     %% calculate the new V value differently depending on the region
     newV(case1) = (1-dt).*V(case1);
     newV(~case1) = (1-dt).*V(~case1) + dt*U(~case1);
     %% enforce boundary conditions by calling the sub-function boundary()
     newU=boundary(newU);
     newV=boundary(newV);
```

```matlab
function X = boundary(X)
%% This subfunction enforces zero gradient at the boundary
    X(:,1) = X(:,2);
    X(:,end) = X(:,end-1);
    X(1,:) = X(2,:);
    X(end,:) = X(end-1,:);

function SimTissue(N, T, stime, ptime, D, dt)
%% this procedure simulates T time steps on an N × N region of tissue
%% every stime steps the tissue will be stimulated at a random location
%% every ptime steps the figure will be updated
%% D sets the diffusion rate and dt sets the time step
    [U,V]=InitTissue(N);
    for t=1:T
        [U,V]=StepTissue(U,V,D,dt);
        if mod(t,stime)==0
            U=StimTissue(U,ceil(rand(1)*N),ceil(rand(1)*N));
        end
        if mod(t,ptime)==0
            figure(1);
            pcolor(U);
            caxis([0 1]);
            colormap copper
            shading interp
            drawnow;
        end
    end

function TestTissue(N, T, stime, r, c, ptime, D, dt)
%% this procedure simulates T time steps on an N × N region of tissue
%% once, at stime steps the tissue will be stimulated at (r,c)
%% every ptime steps the figure will be updated
%% D sets the diffusion rate and dt sets the time step
    [U,V]=InitTissue(N);
    for t=1:T
        [U,V]=StepTissue(U,V,D,dt);
        if t==stime
            U=StimTissue(U,r,c);
        end
        if mod(t,ptime)==0
            figure(1);
            pcolor(U);
            caxis([0 1]);
            colormap copper
            shading interp
            drawnow;
        end
    end
```

II. Interpretation of the Results

Figure A.3 shows what happens under normal heart conditions. The wave begins at the center and runs to the edges and the excitation ends. Figure A.4 shows what happens when we have induced fibrillation by having a second shock shortly after the initial excitation. The image was obtained by shocking a 160 × 160 system a second time 90 steps after the initial excitation at a location slightly off-center (80,90). The secondary shock causes the development of spiral waves that continue to self-generate indefinitely.

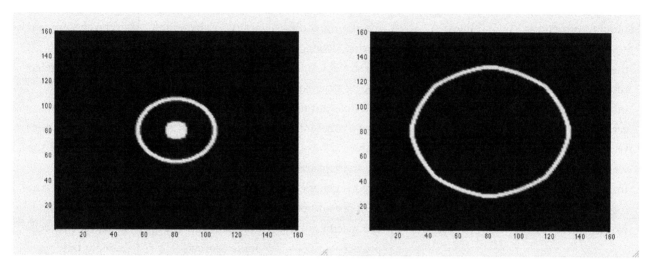

FIGURE A.3 The propagation of a wave as a circular front in the simulated heart tissue. This represents a simulation of normal heart function where waves move regularly through the tissue in a way that terminates after the tissue is fully stimulated.

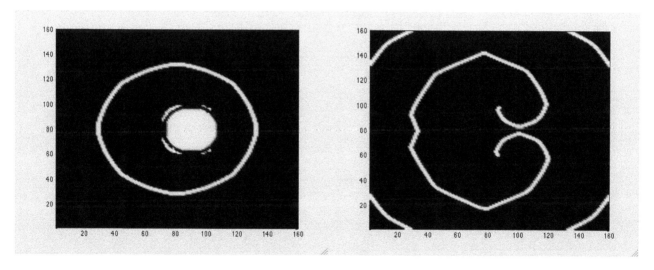

FIGURE A.4 The propagation of a wave interrupted by a second shock inducing fibrillation. Fibrillation is characterized by a spiral wave pattern that never ceases as the spiral continues to trigger a response in the tissue.

ASSESSMENT RUBRICS

TABLE A.1 *Assessment rubric to evaluate students' strategies before getting into the solution*

Criterion	Poor (0–2)	Fair (3–5)	Good (6–8)	Excellent (9–10)
PLANNING/PROGRAM DESIGN Evaluates the student's plan for completing the project. Student Instructions Summarize the nature of the algorithm briefly, identifying the most relevant information from the project description. Articulate a well-thought-out strategy for designing, coding, testing, and debugging your work. (10%)	No strategy is articulated for the design, coding, testing, or debugging.	The strategy provided considers two or fewer of the defined areas (designing, coding, testing, debugging). The strategy is poorly articulated and does not represent a coherent plan. The strategy articulated is generic and does not address the specifics of the project.	The strategy includes all but one of the defined areas (designing, coding, testing, debugging). The nature of the algorithm is not summarized, or the summary does not reference aspects of the project description. The description of the strategy is unclear or misguided in one or more aspects.	All four areas (designing, coding, testing, debugging) are addressed clearly in the context of the project. The summary references the project description and identifies relevant aspects of the project. The strategy is articulated clearly and is logical and well thought out.

TABLE A.2 *Assessment rubric to evaluate students' solutions in terms of product and process*

Criterion	Poor (0–2)	Fair (3–5)	Good (6–8)	Excellent (9–10)
PROGRAM EXECUTION Evaluates the extent to which the program functions in a way that conforms to specifications. Does the program execute? Is the input and output of the expected form? (25%)	The program does not run at all.	The program contains two or more easily correctable syntax errors that impede execution. Program input or output is not as described in the specifications of the project.	The program is free of syntax errors that impede execution. Program takes the expected input parameters and returns the expected output as required in the specification except in minor respects.	The program is free of syntax errors that impede execution. Program takes the expected input parameters and returns the expected output as required in the specification in all respects.
SPECIFICATION SATISFACTION Evaluates the degree to which the solution satisfies the specification. Is the solution accurate and robust? Does it conform to the problem specifications regarding format, order, and presentation? (25%)	The solution produces wholly incorrect output under all of the tests run.	The solution produces incorrect output under a number of the tests. Output is correct, but does not meet specifications in one or more respects.	The solution produces incorrect output in particular cases. Output always meets specifications regarding format, order and presentation when correct.	The solution produces correct output in all cases with only minor exceptions. All output meets specifications regarding format, order, and presentation.
CODING STYLE Measures the extent to which the code is presented in a manner that is clearly readable by others. Is the code indented and commented, and are variable and function names chosen to enhance readability? Does the code appropriately deploy language capabilities to avoid redundant structures, global variables, and unnecessarily lengthy blocks of code? (10%)	Code is entirely uncommented. Global variables are used without justification due to exceptional circumstances. Code is not differentiated into functions or m-files (i.e., spaghetti code).	Code is poorly commented. Code is not properly indented. Variable and function names are chosen without consideration. Code is unnecessarily complex due to the underuse of functions, control constructs, or other language capabilities.	Code is adequately commented. Code is properly indented, and variable and function names are well chosen. Code could be made more readable in one or more ways by additional commenting or by more logically organizing its structure.	Code is well commented. Code is properly indented, and variable and function names are well chosen. Code is well structured.

Continued

TABLE A.2 *Continued*

Criterion	Poor (0–2)	Fair (3–5)	Good (6–8)	Excellent (9–10)
VALIDATION OF THE SOLUTION Establishes whether the proposed solution satisfies the problem's requirements and produces correct output for a range of test cases. Students are expected to run provided test cases and compare them to provide output, as well as propose at least three additional well-chosen test cases for the purpose of validation. (10%)	No evidence of validation. *or* Only provided test cases are run. *or* Test cases are run, but the output is not discussed regarding its implications for validation.	All provided test cases are run, and output is provided. At least one test case is proposed. Comparisons are made between program output and student test cases, and some discussion is provided.	All provided test cases are run, and valid output is provided. Three test cases are proposed, but they are perhaps not well-chosen to test a range of independent solutions, or the answers are not well-justified. Comparisons are made to the student test cases, and these are discussed adequately.	All provided test cases are run, and valid output is provided. Three well-chosen and independent test cases are proposed, and the anticipated output is well-justified. Comparisons are made to the student test cases, and these are passed.
DEPLOYMENT OF DISCIPLINARY CONCEPTS Evaluates whether the student can use the solution to approach a disciplinary problem. Can the student use their code to address the disciplinary issue or to solve a related problem? (20%)	No solution provided.	A solution is provided, but it is incorrect or does not adequately address the issue or problem.	A solution is provided that would adequately address the issue or problem, but it is presented in a way that is unclear or improperly documented (e.g., graphs without axes, no written description when requested).	A solution is provided that is correct, clear, and well documented.

APPENDIX B

Sample Project and Solution for Designing for Capstone Courses

Sections of this appendix and supporting documentation have been previously reported in Lyon and Magana (2021)* and Lyon, Magana, and Streveler (2022).

PROJECT DESCRIPTION

Introduction

You are a team of new project engineers at FOODSCorp. Your engineering team received the following email (figure B.1) regarding a new job your company, FOODSCorp, has been contracted to do. Your engineering team has been given the following information (figures B.1, B.2, and B.3).

-----Original Message-----

From: Jennifer Gonzalez [mailto: jgonzalez@lyoncorp.com]

Sent: Tuesday, March 10, 2017 7:00 AM

To: Purdue Engineering Team

Subject: Sterilization Line Malfunction

Hey FOODSCorp team,

We know we have done work with you before and are confident we will get great results again. Last night one of our heaters before the filler went out for our canning sterilization line. The manufacturer of the filler is unfortunately in Germany and this is a specialty part, so we don't expect to get the new heating element for a couple of months. In addition, we reached out to general machining; however, they, too, cannot generate the new heating element. The line is working about 10k an hour and runs four different products, so anything we can do to get it running again the company is willing to try.

Our hope is within the next two weeks to get the line back up and running by adjusting processing parameters. However, we do not have the capabilities in-house to model the process using MATLAB software. The heating element was originally able to heat the food material prior to canning to 200°F, but the replacement part we found can only achieve a filling temperature of 180°F currently. After the food is canned, it is heated to commercial sterilization and then cooled with water. Our micro team has asked per company policy that we achieve a 12–15 log reduction in microbial load prior to production. Our quality team has asked that we maximize our vitamin B_1 and vitamin C intact in all products.

I've attached a document overviewing the properties of the food materials as well as a blueprint overviewing our production process. Please deliver us an appropriate computational model via MATLAB software that is capable of outputting visuals of the sterilization process for all four food products showing temperature at various points along the radius as a function of time in addition to plots describing micro load and nutrition degradation. This program should also be able to describe optimal conditions for nutrient retention. In addition, if you could inform us of potential additional energy and time costs from our normal process, that would be helpful. The production runs primarily in the midwestern United States.

Thanks!

Jenn

CAUTION: This email originates from outside of FOODSCorp. Please consider carefully whether you should click on any link, open any attachment, or provide any information.

FIGURE B.1 Email prompt given to students that overviews problem statement.

Properties of the food materials and microbes

Production Line Time Breakdown

Food Material	Moisture Content (%)	Can Size (Can #)	Water Activity (a_w)	Percentage of Production (%)
Tomato Soup	81–84	2	.96	42
Apple Sauce	73–77	10	.99	25
Pumpkin Pie Filling	45–50	3	.98	23
Nacho Cheese	80–85	1 tall	.96	10

*Assume a conduction process inside the can.

Kinetic properties of food components

Component	Z-value (°F)	Ea (kcal/mole)	D^{250}-value
Thiamine	47–49	21–27	246.9 min
Ascorbic Acid	48–52	22–24	1.12 days
Cobalamin	46–49	20–24	1.94 days

Kinetic properties of microorganisms

Microorganism	Z-value (°F)	Ea (kcal/mole)	D^{250}-value
C. Botulinum	12–19	64–82	.1–.2 min
C. Perfringens	15–19	72–79	.02–.04 min
B. Cereus	14–18	65–71	.005–.008 min

Properties of food materials

Food Material	Emissivity	pH	Light Transmittance (%)
Tomato Soup	.87	4.6	5.0
Apple Sauce	.89	3.6	4.0
Pumpkin Pie Filling	.75	5.1	.01
Nacho Cheese	.80	5.8	.05

FIGURE B.2 Modeling parameters for students to build and test their modeled solution.

BLUEPRINT—CANNING PRODUCTION LINE

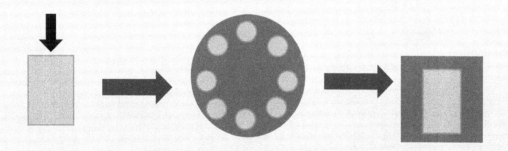

FILLING

Material fill temp: 200°F

Outside room temp: 85°F

FULL STEAM IMMERSION RETORT

Residence time: User selects

Maximum steam temp: 250°F

Maximum rotation speed: 10 RPM

COOLING WATER IMMERSION

Target exit temp: 100°F (average temp in the can)

Cooling water temp: Randomly fluctuates between 50°F and 60°F

FIGURE B.3 Simple system diagram of retort system to be modeled.

Please deliver the following to FOODSCorp as the engineering team that is solving this problem. There will be four deliverables for this assignment.

Deliverable 1: Planning the model template Working with your group, outline the proposed solution in the provided template report (individually). **This will be done during lab time.** During this time, decide which food product each member of the group will model. (Table B.1.)

Deliverable 2: Building the model template/modeling report Individually, complete a building the model template report (provided on Blackboard) using MATLAB Live containing the commented and explained model (bring a printout to class). Each member of the group should code and comment their own model, with each group member modeling the process for one of the four different foods produced. (Table B.2.)

Deliverable 3: Evaluating your model notes Each group will meet with two to three other groups to discuss differences in how they approached the problem, in both a mathematical and a computational sense. An evaluating the model notes template will be provided. **This activity will be completed in class during the first hour of lab time.** (Table B.3.)

Deliverable 4: Reflecting on your model Complete an individual reflection report template that overviews the difference observed from the second in-class activity and allows for reflection as to how your model could be improved or useful in future iterations. (Table B.4.)

TABLE B.1 *Template: In-class activity for planning for the model*

In-class activity (individual working with group): Planning the model	
What properties are needed/not needed for the model? For each food property, give reasoning as to why.	
Food property:	Why is/is not used:
How do you intend to address each property where a range or raw data is given in the final model? For each property listed, please give reasoning as to why you are choosing your current strategy.	
Food property:	How will you use or address it? Why?

TABLE B.1 *Continued*

Are there food properties needed that are not given in the problem statement? If any, please justify why they are needed and what source you will obtain them from.		
Food property needed:	Why is it needed?	Why did you use the source you did?

What assumptions will you make to solve the problem? For each assumption, explain why you made it and what it may limit about your model.		
Assumption:	Why did you choose it?	What will this limit?

Provide the mathematical equations necessary to solve the problem. For each equation, please explain why it was chosen and any assumptions your model will make about it. Please list all equations necessary. Feel free to use the course textbook or online materials.		
Equation needed:	Why is this needed?	What assumptions does this equation make?

What computational technique will you use to solve the system? Explain why this technique was chosen, what the benefits are, and what the limitations are (e.g., implicit finite difference, explicit finite difference, finite element method, Crank-Nicolson method, Monte Carlo method).
Computational technique chosen:
What are the benefits of this technique?
What are the limitations of this technique?
Why did you choose this technique over alternatives?

TABLE B.2 *Template: Take-home assignment for building the model*

Take-home assignment (individual): Building the model	
Please outline and describe how your model works in terms of computational structures. For each structure, please explain why the programming technique or process used was chosen. Include as much detail as possible, doing this for each computational structure within your model (e.g., groups of variables, loops, conditional statements, sets of equations).	
Computational structure:	How does it work? Why was it programmed this way?
Ex. Nested for loop in lines 15–25 of function X.	Ex. The nested for loop indexes through both rows and columns to move through both time and space. It was used because there was a set endpoint, thus it was more efficient than a while loop that exits upon an unknown number of iterations. This is useful given it is unknown how long heat will take to transfer.
Ex. Define thermal variables in lines 26–33.	Ex. These statements define how heat moves through the material. These variables are necessary to be defined previous to the equations in line 45 as they are used there. Variable X does ... and interacts with variable Y in this way ...

Please describe any assumptions made during the modeling process and why those may have been good or appropriate assumptions.		
Assumption:	Why did you make this assumption?	How does this impact how your model works?

What process parameters are you using for each of the food materials?
1. What microorganism is your program targeting? All of them? Only one? Why?
2. What is the new time needed to commercially sterilize the product and the time needed to cool the product to the required average temperature?

TABLE B.2 *Continued*

3. What optimum temperatures were used for sterilization to retain nutrients? How do you know this is the optimum? Compare the optimum between the original (200°F fill temperature) with the alternate (180°F fill temperature).
4. Insert a graph of the heating and cooling profile of the center of the can during the process. How do specific physical properties of the food impact this graph?
5. Insert a graph of the biological activity profile in the product at the center of the can vs. time. Why would the center of the can make the most sense to monitor?
6. Insert a graph of the average nutrient activity profile throughout the entire can vs. time. Why would we use the average nutrient content across the can rather than at a single point?
How do parameters such as food composition, thermal properties of the food, geometry (can size), and processing parameters (times and temperatures) seem to impact the heating profile?
How did you test how these properties affected the heating profile?
For your process, how are vitamin B_1 and vitamin C affected? How much of these vitamins remain? How much more vitamin loss is there in the new process (180°F fill temperature) than the original (200°F fill temperature)?
What is your estimate of additional energy and time costs due to the impacted filling temperature for your product?

Continued

TABLE B.2 *Continued*

What recommendations would you make to the systems engineer, R&D, and microbiology to improve costs and efficiencies on this line moving forward?

TABLE B.3 *Template: In-class activity for evaluating the model*

In-class activity (individual with the group): Evaluate your model
Questions to discuss during group rotation meetings. For these meetings, focus on *how* and *why* you solved and programmed the problem the way you did.
1. What are the different assumptions you made about the physical properties of the system? Did you use different data? How would these differences impact the model?
2. Make a line-by-line comparison with the other students' programming files. How did your programming strategies differ? What advantages do you see in how they did their model? What advantages do you see in your own?

TABLE B.4 *Template: Take-home assignment for reflecting on the model*

Take-home assignment (individual): Reflect on your model		
What approaches did other students take with respect to the data they used (justifications, assumptions, and limitations) and the way they programmed their model? Be as detailed as possible in listing various differences between models. For each difference, talk about *why* you think the other students chose to do it the way they did. Be detailed.		
How did these differ from your own approach? When would your own approach make the most sense? When would different assumptions that other groups made make the most sense?		
Differences I saw:	What approach makes the most sense:	Why the approach makes the most sense:
If you were to do this assignment again, what different assumptions would you make, and what do you believe to be the optimal solution to the problem?		
Things I would do differently:	Why I would do them differently:	
What was the most challenging piece of this assignment?		
Why do you think it was the most challenging?		
How did you overcome this challenge?		

PROJECT SOLUTION

I. Example Solution in MATLAB Code

```
clc;
clear;
count=0; %counter variable 1
t=0; %initial time
%Tomato Soup
xw=.8079;
xc=.1412;
xp=.0146;
xft=.0044;
xash=.0209;
xfib=.011;
radius=43.7;%mm
nodes=200;
%Mesh Size
delx=radius/nodes;
delt=.05;%seconds
%Initial Temp
maxcount=1
Tcount=121;
lethal=0; %initial lethality
Tinitial=82;%Celcius
T=zeros(1,nodes);
T=T+Tinitial;
T(1,1)=Tcount;%Celcius
Tnew=zeros(1,nodes);
%Kinetics of C bot.
D250=.2;%min
D250seconds=.2*60;%seconds
Zvalue=15;%F
Ea=73;%kcal/mole
ZvalueC=15*5/9;%C
heatcycle=0;
xxx=0;
while xxx<2
     if lethal<12
while lethal<12
alpha = choiokos(xc, xp, xw, xft, xfib, xash, T );
%Check for stability
M=(delx^2)./(alpha.*delt);
if min(M<4)
     print('solution became unstable');
     return
end
```

```
for n=2:1:nodes
Tnew(1)=T(1,1);
if n<nodes
     Tnew(n)=(1./M(n)).*(((2.*n+1)./(2.*n)).*T(n+1)+(M(n)-
2).*T(n)+((2.*n-1)./(2.*n)).*T(n-1));
else
     Tnew(n)=(4./M(n)).*T(n-1)+((M(n)-4)/M(n)).*T(n);
End
end
%display(Tnew(nodes))
t=t+delt;
count=count+1;
tvec_center(count)=t;
Tvec_center(count)=Tnew(nodes);
T=Tnew;
Ksterile=1*D250seconds*10^((121-Tvec_center(count))./Zvalue);
lethal_new=2.303./(Ksterile).*delt;
lethal=lethal+lethal_new;
display(lethal)
end
tsterilize=t;
     else
T(1,1)=15;%C cooling water
Taverage=39;
while Taverage>38; %C
alpha = choiokos(xc, xp, xw, xft, xfib, xash, T );
M=(delx^2)./(alpha.*delt);
T(1,1)=15;
Taverage=T(1)*(3.14*((nodes-1)*delx)^2-(3.14*((nodes-2)*delx)^2))/
(3.14*(delx*(nodes-1)^2));
for n=2:1:nodes
if n<nodes
     Tnew(n)=(1./M(n)).*(((2.*n+1)./(2.*n)).*T(n+1)+(M(n)-
2).*T(n)+((2.*n-1)./(2.*n)).*T(n-1));
     Taverage=Taverage+Tnew(n)*(((3.14*((nodes-n)*delx)^2)-
(3.14*(((nodes-n-1)
*delx)^2))))/(((((nodes-1)*delx)^2)*3.14);
else
     Tnew(n)=(4./M(n)).*T(n-1)+((M(n)-4)/M(n)).*T(n);
End
end
t=t+delt;
count=count+1;
tvec_center(count)=t;
Tvec_center(count)=Tnew(nodes);
T=Tnew;
end
     end
```

```
xxx=xxx+1;
Tcountvector(maxcount)=Tcount;
maximizetimevector(maxcount)=t;
maxcount=maxcount+1;
end
formatspec='The time to sterilize is %f minutes';
fprintf(formatspec, tsterilize./60)
formatspec2='The total time is %f minutes';
fprintf(formatspec2, t./60)
plot(tvec_center./60,Tvec_center)
%formatspec3='The optimum sterilzation temperature is %f degrees C';
%fprintf(formatspec3, max(Tcountvector))
```

II. Interpretation of the Results

Figures B.4, B.5, B.6, and B.7 show how the temperature changes in the center of the can for various systems provided to the teams (different foods and sized cans). In each figure, as the temperature rises in the can the material continues to be sterilized. The curve then takes a sharp downward turn as cooling begins. This results in two pieces of information for each team: the total time to sterilize (temperature rising) and total time including cooling (from beginning to final time).

1. Tomato soup heating profile at center at 121°C heating condition in radius 43 mm can.

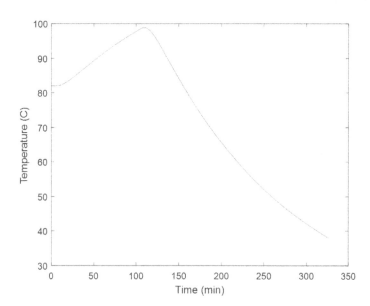

FIGURE B.4 Temperature change as a function of time at the center of 43 mm can of tomato soup.

The time to sterilize 100.7 minutes. Total time is 326 minutes.

2. Apple sauce heating profile at center at 121°C heating condition in radius 78 mm can (num 10).

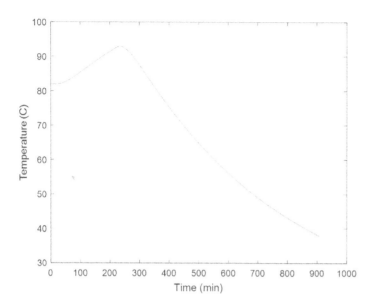

FIGURE B.5 Temperature change as a function of time at the center of 78 mm can of apple sauce.

The time to sterilize is 203 minutes. Total time is 904 minutes.

3. Pumpkin pie filling heating profile at center at 121°C heating condition in radius 54 mm can.

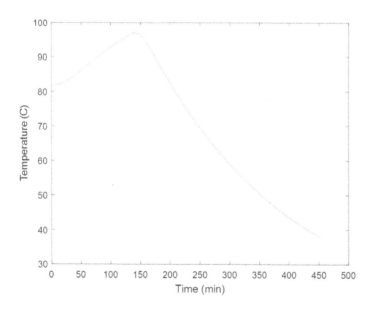

FIGURE B.6 Temperature change as a function of time at the center of 54 mm can of pie filling.

The time to sterilize is 127 minutes. Total time is 450 minutes.

4. Nacho cheese heating profile at center at 121°C heating condition in radius 34.29 mm can.

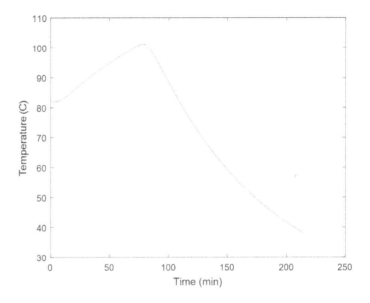

FIGURE B.7 Temperature change as a function of time at the center of 34.29 mm can of cheese sauce.

The time to sterilize is 73 minutes. Total time is 214 minutes.

ASSESSMENT RUBRIC

TABLE B.5 *Assessment rubric to evaluate students' implementation and solutions*

Learning Objective	Unsuccessful (0)	Successful (5)	Above Successful (10)
Students are able to identify useful data and justify its use. (15%) ARTIFACT Solution proposal (week 1); students are asked to set up the problem using information from the problem statement.	Students use pieces of irrelevant data with an irrational or missing justification for its use.	Students correctly identify relevant data; however, they have irrational or missing justifications.	Students correctly identify relevant data and rationally justify its use.
Students are able to convert mathematical representations of information into appropriate computational structures and justify their choice. (30%) ARTIFACT Student m.files (week 2) that are required to have in-code comments justifying each line of code.	Students are not successful in interpreting mathematical structures in relation to computational abstractions.	Students successfully interpret mathematical structures in relation to computational abstractions.	Students successfully interpret mathematical structures in relation to computational abstractions and justify appropriateness and efficiency of choice.

TABLE B.5 *Continued*

Learning Objective	Unsuccessful (0)	Successful (5)	Above Successful (10)
Students are able to construct computational models from identified information and develop computational structures. (30%) ARTIFACT Student final report (week 2) that requires an outline of the model, answers to specific discipline questions, and presentation to the class.	The computational model does not function/has multiple errors or does not answer the identified question.	The computational model functions properly with minimal errors. The model provides reasonable answers to the identified question.	The computational model functions with no errors and provides a relevant answer to the identified question.
Students are able to interpret modeling output in relation to the problem context. (15%) ARTIFACT Student evaluation report (week 3) asks for an interpretation of own model and for results from class discussion around other approaches to the same problem obtained from week 2 presentations.	Student either fail to provide other approaches or incorrectly interpret their own approach.	Students provide other approaches but fail to identify the strengths and weaknesses of each approach in relation to their own.	Students provide a correct interpretation of their own approach, in addition to other approaches, and a comparison of the strengths and weaknesses of each approach is created.
Students are able to reflect on their learning experiences and discuss what they would do differently in the future. (10%) ARTIFACT Student reflection report (week 4) that asks students to discuss what they would do differently in the future and the benefits and drawbacks of their approach.	Student either fail to provide detailed challenges or fail to identify areas of improvement.	Students identify challenges and weaknesses of their approach but fail to identify the reasoning as to why it was a weakness or the reasoning for taking a new approach.	Students are able to identify the challenges of their approach, what they would do differently in the future, and why they would change their approach.

APPENDIX C

Sample Project and Solution for Designing for Learning in the Laboratory

THE DESIGN OF THE COMPUTATIONAL LABORATORY ASSIGNMENTS WAS BASED ON learning materials created by professors Sanjay Rebello and Carina Rebello, with the help of Yuri Piedrahita, at Purdue University.

PROJECT DESCRIPTION

LAB 2: Position, Velocity, and Acceleration

Goal: After completing this activity, you should be able to

- Use loops to model motion iteratively in VPython.
- Measure 1D position, velocity, and acceleration.
- Connect physical experiment and a VPython model.

I. Iterative Vector Modeling

A loop is a set of code instructions that repeatedly runs until some condition is met. In VPython, one example of a loop is the while loop (figure C.1).

A while loop starts with a condition (e.g., $x < 10$) followed by commands that are executed as long as that condition is met. When the condition is no longer met (e.g., $x \geq 10$), the program moves on to the line of code following the loop. Notice that all of the instruction lines are indented one tab past the while condition. This tells GlowScript what

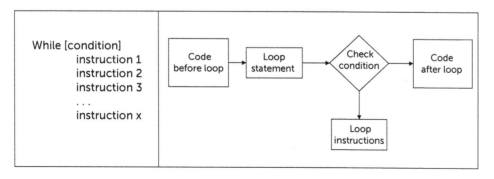

FIGURE C.1 Example of a while loop.

lines of code are contained within the while loop. Returning to standard non-indented lines indicates the end of the loop. Let's look at an actual example in VPython.

1. From any internet browser, go to http://www.glowscript.org.
2. Sign in with your Google account (e.g., Gmail, YouTube).
3. Open your programs by clicking on "Your programs are here."
4. Open your Public folder. You should see your programs from Lab 1.
5. In your Public folder, create a new program called Loops.
6. Click on the following link and copy the code from WhileLoopTutorial into your new Loops.py program: https://www.glowscript.org/#/user/HaydenFennell /folder/Lab2/. (*Note:* The code is provided in full at the end of this appendix.)
7. Uncomment Part 1 by removing one # before each sentence. Lines with ## will continue to remain as comments.
8. Examine the code and read through the comments following each line to determine what the code is doing.

    Q: How many times do you predict that the loop in Part 1 will execute? Explain why.

    Q: Run the code. How many times does the code run? Does this match your prediction?

9. Re-comment Part 1 of the code by adding one # in front of each line. Uncomment Part 2.
10. Examine the code and read through the comments after each line to determine what the code is doing.

    Q: What is the conditional statement checking in Loop 2?

    Q: How many times do you predict that the loop in Part 2 will execute?

    Q: Run the code. How many times does the code run? Does this match your prediction?

II. Pushcart VPython Simulation

Now you will use loops to model motion using the position update formula:
$\vec{r}_f = \vec{r}_i + \vec{v}\Delta t$.

    Q: How do you think we can use while loops to predict the motion of an object using position update?

Next, we analyze a computational model of pushcart that you will use in the next section. In the simulation, the cart is moving along the track for 2 meters at a constant velocity.

1. In your Public GlowScript folder, create a new program called PushCartSimulation.
2. Copy the code from the following link into your new program: https://www.glowscript.org/#/user/HaydenFennell/folder/Lab2/. (*Note:* The code is provided in full at the end of this appendix.)
3. Carefully review the PushCartSimulation code.
4. Add comments to the code to explain what each part does.

   Q: Which section of the code models the motion of our pushcart? Explain why.

5. Run the code and observe what happens.

   Q: At what time after starting the simulation does the pushcart pass the 1-meter mark?

6. Modify the code so that it provides a more accurate estimate of the time at 1 meter.

   Q: Describe below what changes you made to the code. Explain why. (*Hint:* Think about the experiment with the physical cart-and-rail device. What did you modify to change how often data was recorded by the system?)

   Q: How does the rate at which we record (or generate) data influence our results?

7. Now imagine that our simulation was tracking the motion of a proton being accelerated through a linear particle accelerator.

   Q: If we wanted to accurately estimate the time at which the proton passes through a specific checkpoint in the accelerator, what might need to differ from the pushcart example above? Why?

III. Pushcart Physical Experiment

You will now compare the VPython simulation above with a *real* experiment.

1. Plug the motion sensor into the interface.
2. Open the PASCO Capstone program and check that the motion sensor is detected.
3. Set three graphs to measure position, velocity, and acceleration vs. time simultaneously.
   a. Open a graph display: Double-click on the Graph button on the display bar at the right side of the screen.
   b. Add two new plot areas to the graph display. Click on the Correspond tool on the top bar in the graph display.
   c. Select the measurements for each plot in the graph display. Time on the horizontal axis; position, velocity, and acceleration on the vertical. (Click on the <Select Measurement> button beside the axes and select the respective measurements.)

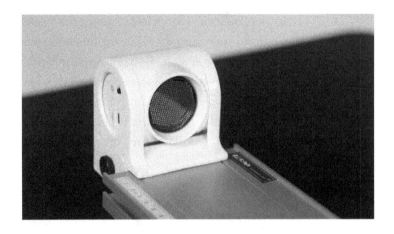

FIGURE C.2 Dynamic cart track with motion sensor.

4. Dock the motion sensor on one extreme of the dynamic cart track as shown in figure C.2.

5. Put the dynamic cart on the track in the opposite extreme of the motion sensor. Make sure the vertical metal sheet in the cart is facing straight toward the motion sensor.

6. Make sure the motion sensor is adjusted in cart mode, selecting the cart symbol with the top button on the motion sensor.

7. With the dynamic cart and the motion sensor at opposite extremes on the track, start to collect data by clicking on the Record button in the control bar at the bottom of the screen. Just after you start to record, give a gentle push on the dynamic cart such that it starts to move at a kind of constant velocity. Stop the recording after a little while.

8. Analyze with your colleagues the three different paths in each plot (position, velocity, and acceleration) as shown in figure C.3.

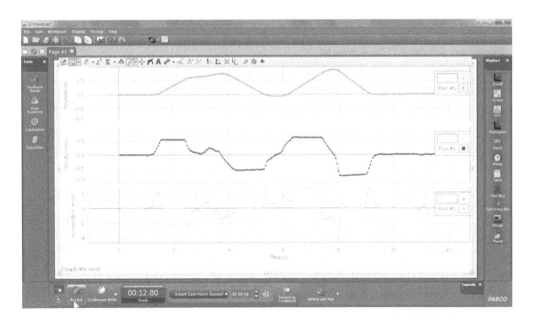

FIGURE C.3 Graph plotting the position, velocity, and acceleration.

Q: Identify in the velocity graph an interval of time where the velocity of the cart was approximately constant. (*Hint:* If your data is too irregular, you can use the Smoothing tool as shown in figure C.7, located on the toolbar in the graph display, to smooth the data of your experiment so that you can easily decide in which period of time the path is closest to constant velocity.) What interval of time is that?

9. Take a screenshot of the relevant portion of the velocity vs. time graph and upload it (one per group).

Q: Looking at the position graph on the screen, what are the initial and final positions of the dynamic cart in the period of time that you chose in the last question? It is the period when the cart moved with constant velocity. (*Hint:* You can find the mean of the collected data, using the tool to calculate statistics of the active data. Click on the Σ button in the toolbar at the top of the graph display. *Note:* To select a specific interval of data, you need to use the tool Highlight Range in the same toolbar used in the last item.)

10. Take a screenshot of the relevant portion of the position vs. time graph and upload it (one per group).

IV. Connecting the VPython Model with the Physical Experiment

Now that you have collected data in a real experiment to measure position, velocity, and acceleration, it is possible to modify the computational model from Part 2 to represent the physical experiment during the period of time that you identified as constant velocity.

1. Take your code from the pushcart program and copy it into a new file in your Public folder (call this program PushCartSimulation2).
2. Adjust the numerical values in the code to model the physical experiment done with the dynamic cart, during the period where the cart had a motion with constant velocity.
3. Compare the graphs obtained in the real experiment with the ones obtained with the new model in VPython and answer the questions below.

Q: How do the two graphs—VPython model and physical experiment—differ from each other?

Q: What assumptions about the cart system does the computational model make? Are these valid assumptions?

Q: How do these assumptions affect the accuracy of our results? For the pushcart simulation, are these assumptions negligible? Why or why not?

4. To conclude today's lab, each student must create share the link to their finished programs.

Q: To share your programs, simply navigate to your Public folder tab and copy the URL from the browser bar into the space below.

LAB 3: Changing Momentum: Measuring Velocity and Force

Goal: After completing this activity, you should be able to

- Measure force and velocity of a fan-cart system.
- Use loops to model change of momentum due to a constant force.
- Connect physical experiment and VPython model.

I. Fan-Cart Physical Experiment

1. Plug the motion and force sensors into the interface(s).
2. Open the PASCO Capstone program and check that the sensors are detected.
3. Dock the motion sensor at one end of the track and put the cart with fan on the track about 15 cm from the motion sensor as shown in figure C.4.
4. Make sure the motion sensor is in cart mode by selecting the cart symbol with the top button on sensor.
5. Set three graphs to measure position, velocity, and acceleration vs. time simultaneously as shown in figure C.5.
6. Double click the Graph button. Add two new plot areas to the graph display.
7. Start to collect data by clicking on the Record button in the control bar in the bottom of the screen. Just after you start to record, turn on the fan such that the cart starts moving *away* from the sensor. Be sure to stop the cart with your hand before it reaches the end. Then stop recording.
8. Observe the three different graphs (position, velocity, and acceleration).

    Q: Identify on the *velocity* graph an interval of time where the velocity is increasing *linearly*. (*Hint:* If your data is too irregular, you can use the Smoothing tool on the toolbar in the graph display to smooth the data.) What interval of time is that? What is the slope of the velocity vs. time graph in that time interval? (*Hint:* You can fit the portion of the graph to a linear

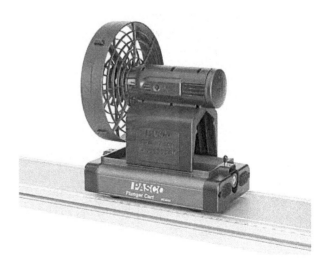

FIGURE C.4 Cart with a fan on the track.

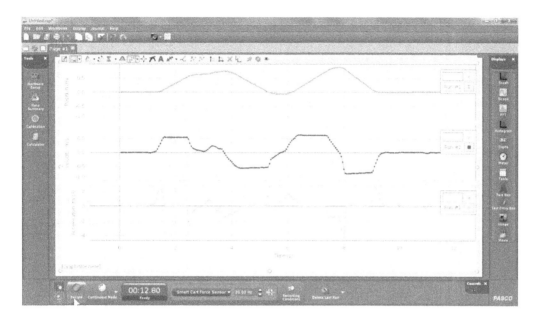

FIGURE C.5 Graph plotting the position, velocity, and acceleration.

curve and find the slope. *Note:* To select a specific interval of data, you need to use the tool Highlight Range in the same toolbar used in the last item.)

Q: Measure the mass of the cart–fan system with a scale and using the momentum principle and the data that you recorded above, to calculate the force exerted by the fan (assume negligible friction). (*Hint:* Momentum principle: $\Delta \vec{p} = \vec{F}_{net}\Delta t \rightarrow m\Delta\vec{v} = \vec{F}_{net}\Delta t \rightarrow \vec{F}_{net} = m(\Delta\vec{v}/\Delta t).$)

9. Now you will compare your calculation above with a measurement. Set a new graph display to measure force vs. time. Open a graph display: Double-click on the Graph button on the display bar. When the graph display is open, select Force (N) in <SelectMeasurement>.

10. Dock the fan on the cart, and connect the cart to the force sensor with a string. Push the ZERO button on the force sensor when the string is relaxed, as shown in figure C.6.

11. Turn on the fan and hold the cart at rest by holding the force sensor until another group member clicks Record. The string is connected to the force sensor, and you are holding the cart stationary by holding the force sensor as shown in figure C.7, so the sensor measures the force exerted by the fan. Stop recording when the force is stable for a few seconds. (*Note:* The resolution of the force sensor is 0.03N.)

   Q: What is the *measured* force? How does it compare with the *calculated* force? What might cause any discrepancies?

FIGURE C.6 ZERO button on the force sensor.

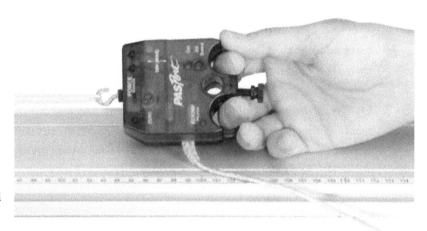

FIGURE C.7 String connected
to the force sensor.

II. Revisiting Computational Models

You will update the Lab 2 simulation (original, *before* you modified it) to model this week's experiment.

1. Go to www.glowscript.org. In your Public folder, create a new program called FanCartSim. Copy and paste the code from the following link in FanCartSim: https://www.glowscript.org/#/user/HaydenFennell/folder/Lab3/. (*Note:* The code is provided in full at the end of this appendix.)

   Q: Last week, you updated only position, not momentum. Why was that? Why must you update momentum now?

2. Now you will modify the above code. Recall that momentum and position updates can be used iteratively:

   Momentum update: $\vec{p}_f = \vec{p}_i + \vec{F}_{net}\Delta t \;\rightarrow\; m\vec{v}_f = m\vec{v}_i + \vec{F}_{net}\Delta t \;\rightarrow\; \vec{v}_f = \vec{v}_i + \left(\frac{\vec{F}_{net}}{m}\right)\Delta t$

   Position update: $\vec{r}_f = \vec{r}_i + \left(\frac{\vec{p}_f}{m}\right)\Delta t \;\rightarrow\; \vec{r}_f = \vec{r}_i + \vec{v}_f\Delta t$

Q: Change the code to accommodate momentum update. Comment the changes that you make.

Q: What new variables/factors need to be taken into account? (*Note:* Remember that when you use new variables, you usually define them at the beginning of the program.)

Q: What sections of the code need to be changed? What sections of the code stay the same?

Q: Fix the parameters of your program to model the experiment of the cart–fan during the interval of linear velocity increment that you chose in the experimental part (initial time, initial position, initial velocity, deltaT, total time). Compare the simulation graphs with those from the experiment. How are they similar? How are they different?

Q: What assumptions about the cart system does the computational model make?

Q: How do these assumptions affect the accuracy of our results? For the pushcart simulation (last week), are these assumptions valid? Why or why not?

LAB 8 Baking Cups Falling: Air Resistance

Goal: After completing this activity, you should be able to

- Measure the position and velocity of a baking cup falling.
- Determine the drag coefficient C of the baking cup from its terminal velocity.
- Use the drag coefficient C and other parameters from the physical experiment to create a VPython model of the baking cup falling.
- Connect physical experiment and VPython model.

I. Falling Cupcake Physical Experiment

1. Using a cellphone, make two videos of baking cups falling vertically from a height of L (see figures C.8 and C.9). If your group number is even, make the videos of one cup falling and three cups falling together. If your group number is odd, make the videos of two cups falling and four cups falling. The L value is up to you; it should be between 1.5 and 2.0 meters. You can do this in the hall outside the room. Make sure the videos cover the same height from top to bottom of the image on your cellphone screen and the height from which you release the cups is the same. You can use the long ruler to keep the height constant in both videos. Make sure you are recording in the middle of the total distance traveled by the cup, and remember to measure the value of the distance L (you should have the cellphone plane completely parallel to the baking cup falling plane), as shown in figure C.9.

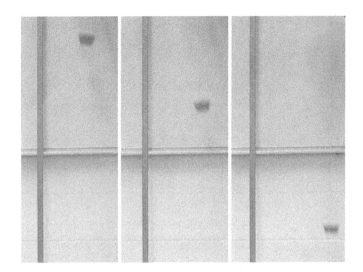

FIGURE C.8 Snapshots of baking cups falling.

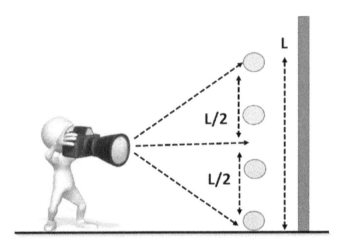

FIGURE C.9 Diagram demonstrating the recording of a falling object.

2. Download your video onto the lab computer.

3. Open the program PASCO Capstone and open a video analysis display (double-click on the Video Analysis tool). Click on Open Movie File and open your video of the baking cup falling.

4. The video should appear on the video analysis display with two yellow tools: the Coordinates tool (x and y axes) and the Calibration tool. The Coordinates tool determines the direction of the position change that the video analysis will measure. The Calibration tool indicates the real scale of the measurements to analyze. Drag the Calibration tool to cover the total distance traveled by the baking cup when it is falling. Adjust the Coordinates tool such that the position of the baking cup falling is measured as positive. Make sure the horizontal axis of the Coordinates tool matches with one of the extremes of the Coordinates tool. (This guarantees that the vertical measurements start in an initial position equal to zero.)

5. Set the real distance traveled by the cup in the Calibration tool. To do that, click on the 1.00 m that appears on one of the ends of the Calibration tool and change that value to the real distance traveled by the cup.

6. The video analysis software permits you to run the video frame by frame when you click the mouse. If the resolution of your video is 240 frames per second, it will take too long to analyze your video. In that case, change the number of frames per click to a reasonable number. To do that, identify the frames per second of your video file by clicking again in the Properties tool, click on Movie Playback, and read the value in Playback Frame Rate. If that number is greater than 30, you need to adjust the frame increment number in the option Overlay. For a playback frame rate of 240, you need to set the frame increment to 5. This means that when you are tracking the motion of the cup in video analysis, each time you click the mouse, five frames of the video will play. If your video has only 30 to 60 frames per second, you do not need to change the frame increment.

7. Add one graph display. Set the <SelectMeasurement> of the graph in Video Analysis → Object #1 → xy, Object # 1 (m/s) vs. Time. You will measure the velocity of the cup vs. time. After setting the graph, play the video until the moment when you release the cup. Put the cursor on the center of the cup and start to track its path as it falls. When a cross appears on the cup, click the mouse and wait until the cup moves to the next position. An example of this process is shown in figure C.10. After each click, you can see how the graph is showing the data collected in the video analysis. Insert a table to visualize the data collected.

FIGURE C.10 Tracking the position of the object (i.e., baking cup) as it descends.

8. You can smooth the curve using the Smoothing tool in the toolbar.

   Q: Look at the velocity graph and discuss with your team members whether the graphs make sense. Summarize your comments. What is the value of the terminal velocity in the graph? (Recall that terminal velocity is the velocity achieved when the weight of the cup equals the drag resistance of the air on the cup.)

9. Repeat the last procedure with the second video with two or four cups falling depending on your group number (two cups for an even group number, four cups

for an odd group number). You need to start by opening a video analysis display (double-click on the Video Analysis tool). It will appear in a window. Click on <Create New Run>, then click on OK. From that point, you can proceed as you did for the first video.

    Q: What is the value of the terminal velocity in your second video?

10. To find the drag coefficient C, you need to use the terminal velocity values of your even/odd neighbor group.

    Q: What are the terminal velocity values of your even/odd neighbor group in their two videos?

11. Measure the mass of a baking cup and make a graph of mass m *(kg)* vs. terminal velocity squared $v^2 \left(\frac{m^2}{s^2} \right)$. The resistance force is $F_d \approx \frac{1}{2} C A \rho v^2$, where C is the drag coefficient, A is the transversal area of the baking cup, ρ is the air density in the classroom, and v is the terminal velocity of the falling cup.

    Q: Given the information about the air resistance force and with the graph of m *(kg)* vs. $v^2 \left(\frac{m^2}{s^2} \right)$, how can you find the value for the drag coefficient C? Describe your procedure.

    Q: Calculate the value for the drag coefficient C.

12. Using the video data collected and Excel, graph the *velocity vs. time* for one, two, three, and four baking cups falling in the same graph so that you can compare them. (Use the data of your neighbor group to complete the data you did not collect in your two videos.)

    Q: Add the graph of the four curves of *velocity vs. time* to your final handout and submit it together via Blackboard.

    Q: Discuss with your team members the graph of the four *velocity vs. time* curves. Are all of them different? Do they make sense? Why or why not?

II. Computational Model of the Baking Cup Falling

You will now use VPython to model the falling baking cup that you analyzed in the physical experiment.

1. Go to www.glowscript.com. In your Public folder, create a new program called AirResistanceSim.
2. Follow the link below and copy and paste the code from AirResistanceSim into your new program: https://www.glowscript.org/#/user/HaydenFennell/folder /Lab8/. (*Note:* The code is provided in full at the end of this appendix.)
3. Read through the code carefully. Comment these lines in your code, indicating what they do.
4. Identify the lines of code that accomplish (a) *velocity* (or momentum) update,

(b) *position* update, and (c) *force* update. Add comments to your code explaining what each of these lines do.

> **Q:** Write down the line numbers of the code associated with (a), (b), and (c).

> **Q:** Run the code and observe what happens. What is the terminal velocity of the simulated cup? How long does it take to reach this velocity?

> **Q:** Change the size (diameter) of your baking cup. What effect does this have on terminal velocity? Report each value you used in your answer.

> **Q:** Change the size (diameter) to its original value, and now change the mass of the cup. What effect does this have on terminal velocity? Change the value of the mass to its original value and try changing the initial height as well. Does this impact your results? Report each value for mass and height in your answer.

5. Now you will modify the code to reflect the values found during today's experiment.
6. Change the parameters of the simulation to use your values from your experimental data collection (drag coefficient *C*, initial time, initial velocity, cup's mass, density of the air, area of the cup, etc.)

> **Q:** What assumptions does the simulation make about the falling cup? How do these assumptions affect the data? (*Hint:* Think about how shape affects your results.)

> **Q:** Compare simulation vs. experiment for *velocity vs. time*. How are they similar? How are they different?

> **Q:** Suppose that the baking cup that you were dropping was conical in shape. What would need to change in the simulation to represent this difference? How would you expect the graphs to change?

PROJECT SOLUTION

Lab 2 VPython Template
GlowScript 2.7 VPython

```
from __future__ import division
from visual import *
###----------------------------------------------------------------
----------------------------###
#Please provide detailed comments explaining the purpose/function of each
line of code in the program below.
```

```
#Be sure to scroll down after running your program to view all of the
output data.
###--------------------------------------------------------------------
-----------------------------###
#Parameters of Simulation (all units are in meters and seconds)
velocity = vector(0.3,0,0)
initialDisplacement = 0
startPosition = vector(initialDisplacement,0,0)
distanceTraveled = 0
totalDistance = 1
t = 0
totalTime = 10
deltaT = 0.5
###------------------Objects in Simulation--------------------###
#This section sets up the visual elements used in the simulation
#You are not required to comment the following section.
###--------------------------------------------------------------###
scene=display(center=vector((totalDistance/2),0,0), background=color.white)
#set the background color
cartTrack=box(pos=vector((totalDistance/2),0,0),
size=vector(totalDistance,0.01,0.05), color=color.black) #Pushcart track
(scales to totalDistance)
pushCart=cone(pos=(startPosition+vector(0,0.05,0)), axis=vector(1,0,0),
radius=0.05, length=0.1, color=color.red) #Pushcart at starting position
label(pos=vector(0,-0.05,0), text="Start", color=color.blue) #Start Line
label(pos=vector(totalDistance,-0.05,0), text="End", color=color.blue) #2
meter marker
scene.autoscale=0 #turn off camera scaling
gd=graph(xtitle='time (s)', ytitle='position (m)') #create graph object
plt=gcurve(color=color.cyan, label='position') #create curve
gd2=graph(xtitle='time (s)', ytitle='velocity (m/s)') #create graph object
plt2=gcurve(color=color.red, label='velocity') #create curve
###------------------End of Objects Section--------------------###
#Please resume commenting for the lines below
###--------------------------------------------------------------###
while (t < totalTime and distanceTraveled < totalDistance):
rate(5) #The rate(n) command tells the computer to halt computation for 1/n
seconds before proceeding. This allows us to slow down the visual refresh
rate of the simulation so that we can actually perceive the motion.
pushCart.pos = pushCart.pos + velocity * deltaT
distanceTraveled = pushCart.pos.x
t = t + deltaT
print("The pushcart is",distanceTraveled,"meters down the track at",
t,"seconds.")
plt.plot(t, distanceTraveled)
plt2.plot(t, velocity.x)
```

Lab 3 VPython Template
GlowScript 2.7 VPython

```
from __future__ import division
from visual import *
###-----------------------------------------------------------------
-----------------------------###
#Please provide detailed comments explaining the purpose/function of each
line of code in the program below.
#Be sure to scroll down after running your program to view all of the
output data.
###-----------------------------------------------------------------
-----------------------------###
#Parameters of Simulation (all units are in meters and seconds)
velocity = vector(0.3,0,0)
initialDisplacement = 0
startPosition = vector(initialDisplacement,0,0)
distanceTraveled = 0
totalDistance = 1
t = 0
totalTime = 10
deltaT = 0.5
###-----------------Objects in Simulation--------------------###
#This section sets up the visual elements used in the simulation
#You are not required to comment the following section.
###--------------------------------------------------------###
scene=display(center=vector((totalDistance/2),0,0), background=color.white)
#set the background color
cartTrack=box(pos=vector((totalDistance/2),0,0),
size=vector(totalDistance,0.01,0.05), color=color.black) #Pushcart track
(scales to totalDistance)
pushCart=cone(pos=(startPosition+vector(0,0.05,0)), axis=vector(1,0,0),
radius=0.05, length=0.1, color=color.red) #Pushcart at starting position
label(pos=vector(0,-0.05,0), text="Start", color=color.blue) #Start Line
label(pos=vector(totalDistance,-0.05,0), text="End", color=color.blue) #2
meter marker
scene.autoscale=0 #turn off camera scaling
gd=graph(xtitle='time (s)', ytitle='position (m)') #create graph object
plt=gcurve(color=color.cyan, label='position') #create curve
gd2=graph(xtitle='time (s)', ytitle='velocity (m/s)') #create graph object
plt2=gcurve(color=color.red, label='velocity') #create curve
###-----------------End of Objects Section--------------------###
#Please resume commenting for the lines below
###--------------------------------------------------------###
while (t < totalTime and distanceTraveled < totalDistance):

rate(5) #The rate(n) command tells the computer to halt computation for 1/n
seconds before proceeding. This allows us to slow down the visual refresh
```

```
rate of the simulation so that we can actually perceive the motion.
pushCart.pos = pushCart.pos + velocity * deltaT
distanceTraveled = pushCart.pos.x
t = t + deltaT
print("The pushcart is",distanceTraveled,"meters down the track at",
t,"seconds.")
plt.plot(t, distanceTraveled)
plt2.plot(t, velocity.x)
```

Lab 8 VPython Template
GlowScript 2.7 VPython

```
from __future__ import division
from visual import *
###------------------------------------------------------------------------
-----------------------------###
#Please provide detailed comments explaining the purpose/function of each
line of code in the program below.
#Be sure to scroll down after running your program to view all of the
output data.
###------------------------------------------------------------------------
-----------------------------###
#Variables of Simulation (all units are in meters and seconds)
mass = 0.005 #kg
g = 9.81 #m/s^2
diameter = 0.1 #m
A = pi * pow((diameter/2), 2) #m^2
rho = 1.225 #kg/m^3
C = 1.15
height = 3 #m
t = 0 #s
totalTime = 10 #s
deltaT = 0.01 #s
initialVelocity = 0 #s
velocity = vector(0,initialVelocity,0)
speed = mag(velocity)
fG = mass*g
fAir = (1/2)*C*rho*A*pow(velocity.y, 2)
fNet = vector(0,(fAir-fG),0)
###------------------------------------------------------------------------
-----------------------------###
```

```
#Visual components of simulation.
#You do not have to edit this section.
#Note that the simulation models the coffee filter as a short cylinder.
###-----------------------------------------------------------------
-------------------------------###
scene=display(center=vector(0,height/2,0), background=color.white) #set the
background color
floor=box(pos=vector(0,0,0), size=vector(2,0.05,0.15), color=color.black)
#Pushcart track (scales to totalDistance)
coffeeFilter=cylinder(pos=vector(0,height,0), axis=vector(0,0.08,0),
radius=diameter/2, color=color.orange) #Pushcart at starting position
scene.autoscale=0 #turn off camera scaling
gd=graph(xtitle='time (s)', ytitle='Distance Fallen (m)') #create graph
object
plt=gcurve(color=color.cyan, label='Distance Fallen') #create curve
gd2=graph(xtitle='time (s)', ytitle='Speed (m/s)') #create graph object
plt2=gcurve(color=color.red, label='Speed') #create curve
###-----------------------------------------------------------------
-------------------------------###
#Simulation code section
###-----------------------------------------------------------------
-------------------------------###
while (coffeeFilter.pos.y > 0 and t < totalTime):
rate(10) #The rate(n) command tells the computer to halt computation for
1/n seconds before proceeding. This allows us to slow down the visual
refresh rate of the simulation so that we can actually perceive the motion.
fAir = (1/2)*C*rho*A*pow(velocity.y, 2)
fNet = vector(0,(fAir-fG),0)
velocity.y = velocity.y + (fNet.y/mass) * deltaT
coffeeFilter.pos.y = coffeeFilter.pos.y + (velocity.y * deltaT)
t = t + deltaT
distanceFallen = height-coffeeFilter.pos.y
speed = mag(velocity)
plt.plot(t, distanceFallen)
plt2.plot(t, speed)
```

ASSESSMENT RUBRICS

TABLE C.1 *Disciplinary scoring rubric*

Category	Below Basic (0)	Basic (1)	Proficient (2)	Advanced (3)
Accuracy of results	Student does not provide results or provides clearly inaccurate results (i.e., results are nonphysical). Student does not provide necessary data (graphs, plots, and/or Excel sheets).	Student provides results, but some results are incorrect. Reported answers conflict with values from data (graphs, plots, and/or Excel data).	Student always provides accurate results. Reported answers agree with values from data (graphs, plots, and/or Excel data).	Student always provides accurate results. *and* Answers speak to the validity of the given results.
Connection and application of results	Student does not provide any connections between the physical and computational models.	Student provides obvious or basic connections (i.e., air resistance, friction, human error).	Student provides obvious or basic connections (i.e., air resistance, friction, human error) but also gives basic explanations of how the specific connections work.	Student provides nonobvious connections (i.e., beyond air resistance, friction) between the physical and computational models similarities and differences.
Quality of results	One-word answers (student does not provide justification and reasoning).	Answers provide minimal/unclear justification of reported values.	Answers provide more detailed justification of the reported values.	Answers provide detailed interpretations that connect to physical principles. Student may also periodically provide analogies or schematic comparisons.

TABLE C.2 *Computational scoring rubric*

Category	Below Basic (0)	Basic (1)	Proficient (2)	Advanced (3)
Accuracy of results	Code does not produce results.	Code produces unreasonable or incorrect results *or* simulation results do not match reported values. Results are inaccurate due to issues within the code (i.e., variables are redefined inappropriately within loop calculations).	Code produces correct results. *and* Simulation results align with reported values.	Code produces correct results. Simulation results align with reported values. Results have been verified/validated against external criteria.
Function and efficiency	Code does not run. *or* Code is needlessly redundant or confusing.	Code functions with minimal warnings or error corrections. Code follows template guidelines, but may include minor inefficiencies (i.e., unnecessarily small step size).	Code functions without error. Code follows template guidelines and uses efficient parameters/settings (i.e., step size is appropriate).	Code functions without error and has been altered to include additional output information. *or* Code includes evidence of monitoring/debugging strategies.
Commenting	No comments. *or* Comments are included, but either indicate a misunderstanding of the code or are confusing or poorly stated.	Comments simply restate the code parameters or simply state variable units. Comments are limited to the variable definition portion of the code *or* code includes less than two quality comments in the body of the program (i.e., the while loop and calculations).	Comments describe the computational function of individual lines or blocks of code in detail. Code includes at least two to three quality comments in the body of the program (i.e., the while loop and calculations).	Comments describe the computational function of individual lines or blocks of code in detail. *and* Comments describe the function of the code in terms of how it represents the disciplinary material

APPENDIX D

Sample Project and Solution for Designing for K–12 Settings

PROJECT DESCRIPTION

This document describes the model Susceptible Infected Recovered (SIR) that represents the spread of an infectious disease. This model is used to describe how a disease (e.g., COVID-19) spreads within a given population and assumes that each individual can be in one of four states:

Susceptible (S): Individuals who have not been infected with the disease, so they are susceptible to being infected within a given probability of disease transmission (i.e., transmission rate) and an average number of contacts per person per time (i.e., contact rate).

Infected (I): Individuals who are infected and can be infectious to others. There is a probability of both recovery and death associated with leaving this state.

Recovered (R): Individuals who were already infected but are now recovered. These individuals cannot be reinfected since they have developed antibodies. (*Note:* This is not necessarily the case for COVID-19, as the evidence about it is inconclusive at this point, but this is the case for other diseases and an assumption of this model.)

Deceased (D): Individuals who were infected and died as a result of the disease.

To identify how many people will move from one state to another, we use the following variables:

Contact rate: Average number of contacts per person per day.

Transmission rate: Probability of disease transmission when a susceptible person comes in contact with an infected person.

Recovery rate: Probability of recovery after being infected.

Mortality rate: Probability of dying after being infected.

Recovery time: Average number of days that the disease stays in the body.

To simulate this model, we need to compute the number of new infections, recoveries, and deaths per day, and then update the number of susceptible, infected, recovered, and deceased as follows:

NewInfections: Infected × Contact rate × (Susceptibles / Total population) × Transmission rate

NewRecoveries: Infected × Recovery rate / Recovery time

NewDeaths: Infected × Mortality rate / Recovery time

Susceptibles: Susceptibles − NewInfections

Infected: Infected + NewInfections − (NewRecoveries + NewDeaths)

Recovered: Recovered + NewRecoveries

Deceased: Deceased + NewDeaths

As one may expect, there are some variables that we can manipulate and see the effects on the number of infected people and the number of deaths. For instance, closing public events and banning large gatherings of people, may decrease the *contact rate*, which has a direct effect on the number of new infections and the number deaths. Likewise, if doctors find effective treatments to the disease, we may have a lower *mortality rate*, which will reduce the number of deaths.

PROJECT TEMPLATES

Sample Jupyter Notebook: Figure D.1 depicts a screenshot of the sample Jupyter Notebook provided to the students for them to complete the SIR model.

FIGURE D.1 Screenshot of a Sample Jupyter Notebook, which shows the Python code initializing the model parameters, a brief explanation, and the incomplete provided example.

https://github.com/cvieiram/introPythonIngenieria/blob/master/Sample%20Jupyter%20Notebook.ipynb

PROJECT SOLUTION

Completed Jupyter Notebook: Figure D.2 shows the screenshot of the solution to the SIR model in a Jupyter Notebook. Figure D.3 shows the Python code that reports the outcomes of the SIR model once the simulation is completed.

FIGURE D.2 Screenshot of the Jupyter Notebook with the full solution to the SIR model.

https://github.com/cvieiram/introPythonIngenieria/blob/master/Completed%20Jupyter%20Notebook.ipynb

```
In [62]:  # This is the solution for the indicators that we are asking students to compute.
          # They will need to understand the simulation in order to compute these accurately
          # Students will need to run the simulation using different values for the
          # variables ContactRate, RecoveryRate, and MortalityRate to make conclusions about the effect of different measures

          print('Total Infections')
          print(sum(listInfected))
          print('Total Recovered')
          print(sum(listRecovered))
          print('Total Unaffected')
          print(TotalPopulation-sum(listInfected))
          print('Total Deaths')
          print(sum(listDeaths))

          print('Max number of people infected in a given date')
          print(maxInfected)
          print('Max number of infections in one day')
          print(max(listInfected))
          print('Max number of recovered people in one day')
          print(max(listRecovered))
          print('Max number of deaths in one day')
          print(max(listDeaths))
```

FIGURE D.3 Screenshot of the section in the Jupyter notebook that reports the outcomes of the model.

https://github.com/cvieiram/introPythonIngenieria/blob/master/Completed%20Jupyter%20Notebook.ipynb

ASSESSMENT RUBRIC

TABLE D.1 *Assessment rubric for the project solution*

Criteria	Poor (0–2)	Fair (3–5)	Good (6–8)	Excellent (9–10)
PROGRAM EXECUTION Evaluates the level of detail and explicitness in the written procedure. Does the program execute correctly? (30%)	Program does not compile or run at all.	Program runs, but mostly incorrectly (correct output 30%–74% of the time).	Program produces correct output most of the time (75% of the time or more).	Program runs correctly.
SPECIFICATION SATISFACTION Evaluates the degree under which the solution satisfies the specification. Is the solution accurate and of high quality? Does it satisfy the problem specifications? (30%)	The solution is incomplete and lacks quality. Program does not satisfy the specifications.	Many parts of the specifications are not implemented. Solution is low quality. Only some of the specifications are satisfied.	Most parts of the solution are accurate (75% or more). Most of it depicts a model of quality. Program satisfies most of the specifications (75%).	The solution is very accurate and of high quality. Program satisfies specifications completely and correctly.
CODING STYLE Measures how well the solution is written. Is the code ease to follow? Does it appropriately use the language capabilities? (10%)	Incomprehensible code. Appropriate language capabilities unused.	Code hard to follow in one reading. Poor use of language capabilities.	Code basically organized. Code does not follow basic coding standards.	Well-formatted, understandable code. Appropriate use of language capabilities.
DEPLOYMENT OF DISCIPLINARY CONCEPTS Evaluates whether the student can use the solution to approach a disciplinary problem. Can the student use their code as applied to some disciplinary problem or to solve some related question? (30%)	There is no solution. The student is not able to apply the solution to the disciplinary problem.	The student is able to roughly align the solution to the disciplinary problem. The student does not fully understand the output.	The student is able to apply the solution to the disciplinary knowledge with certain changes or constraints. The student explains the results but depicts some misconceptions about disciplinary concepts.	The student is able to seamlessly apply the solution to the disciplinary knowledge. The student is able to explain the results in terms of the discipline.

ACKNOWLEDGMENTS

THIS BOOK WOULD NOT HAVE BEEN POSSIBLE WITHOUT THE SUPPORT AND EN-couragement of my beloved husband, Bedrich Benes. You inspired me to pursue this project and continuously motivated me throughout the process.

I am eternally grateful to my former students, now my colleagues, and my collaborators for joining me on this journey. Thank you for entrusting me as your mentor and contributing to the project with your unique expertise as we investigated this topic jointly. More importantly, thank you for sharing your enthusiasm and passion for doing research in this area. Thank you for your significant contributions to this work and the many revisions to each of the chapters.

Thank you to the reviewers, anonymized and named, for your comments and suggested revisions to this manuscript. Thank you, Michael Loui, for your critical comments and insightful feedback that continuously helped me "speak" to engineering educators and researchers. Thank you, Ruth Streveler, for your valuable comments and suggestions that helped improve the connections to theory. Thank you, Brian Hong, for helping me make this content more accessible to practitioners. Also, thank you, Mariana Silva, for piloting the ideas and materials of this book as part of your ongoing professional development efforts. Finally, thank you to all the students and faculty members who participated in the studies. I appreciate all of you taking time from your busy schedules to share your learning experiences and expertise.

This material is based upon work supported in part by the National Science Foundation under award numbers EEC-1449238, EEC-1329262, EEC-1137006, EEC-1826099, CMMI-2134667, DBI-2120200, and DGE-1842166.

REFERENCES

Abeysekera, Lakmal, and Phillip Dawson. 2015. "Motivation and Cognitive Load in the Flipped Classroom: Definition, Rationale and a Call for Research." *Higher Education Research & Development* 34 (1): 1–14. https://doi.org/10.1080/07294360.2014.934336.

ACARA (Australian Curriculum, Assessment and Reporting Authority). n.d. "Understanding How Technologies Works." https://www.australiancurriculum.edu.au/f-10-curriculum/technologies/.

AI4K12. 2020. "The Artificial Intelligence (AI) for K–12 Initiative (AI4K12)." Association for the Advancement of Artificial Intelligence and the Computer Science Teacher Association. https://ai4k12.org/.

Amalia, Fitriana Rizqi, S. Ibnu, H. R. Widarti, and H. Wuni. 2018. "Students' Mental Models of Acid and Base Concepts Taught Using Cognitive Apprenticeship Learning Model." *Journal Pendidikan IPA Indonesia* 7 (2): 187–92. https://doi.org/10.15294/jpii.v7i2.14264.

Arigye, Joreen, Alejandra J. Magana, Joseph A. Lyon, and Elsje Pienaar. 2023. "Biomedical and Agricultural Engineering Undergraduate Students Programming Self-Beliefs and Changes Resulting from Computational Pedagogy." In *Proceedings of the 2023 American Society for Engineering Education Annual Conference & Exposition*. ASEE Conferences. https://peer.asee.org/42275.

Arigye, Joreen, Aabas Udosen, Parth Pravin, and Alejandra J. Magana. 2023. "The Evolution of Team Coordination Commitments in the Context of Computational Projects." Paper presented at the 2023 IEEE ASEE Frontiers in Education Conference. College Station, Texas, October 18–21, 2023.

Azemi, Asad, and Laura L. Pauley. 2006. "Teaching the Introductory Computer Programming Course for Engineers Using Matlab and Some Exposure to C." In *Proceedings of the 2006 American Society for Engineering Education Annual Conference & Exposition*. ASEE Conferences. https://doi.org/10.18260/1-2--670.

Barab, Sasha A., and Kurt Squire. 2004. "Introduction: Design-Based Research: Putting a Stake in the Ground." *Journal of the Learning Sciences* 13 (1): 1–14. https://doi.org/10.1207/s15327809jls1301_1.

Barkley, Dwight. 1991. "A Model for Fast Computer Simulation of Waves in Excitable Media." *Physica D: Nonlinear Phenomena* 49 (1–2): 61–70. https://doi.org/10.1016/0167-2789(91)90194-E.

Bellomo, Nicola, and Luigi Preziosi. 1994. *Modelling Mathematical Methods and Scientific Computation*. CRC Press.

Boblett, Nancy. 2012. "Scaffolding: Defining the Metaphor." *Studies in Applied Linguistics and TESOL* 12 (2). https://doi.org/10.7916/salt.v12i2.1357.

Bowen, G. Michael, Wolff-Michael Roth, and Michelle K. McGinn. 1999. "Interpretations of Graphs by University Biology Students and Practicing Scientists: Toward a Social Practice View of Scientific Representation Practices." *Journal of Research in Science Teaching* 36 (9): 1020–43. https://doi.org/10.1002/(SICI)1098-2736(199911)36:9<1020::AID-TEA4>3.0.CO;2-%23.

Bransford, John D., Ann L. Brown, and Rodney R. Cocking. 2000. *How People Learn: Brain, Mind, Experience, and School (Expanded Edition)*. Washington, DC: National Academy Press.

Braught, Grant, Tim Wahls, and L. Marlin Eby. 2011. "The Case for Pair Programming in the Computer Science Classroom." *ACM Transactions on Computing Education (TOCE)* 11 (1): 2. https://doi.org/10.1145/1921607.1921609.

Brophy, Sean P., and Sensen Li. 2010. "A Framework for Using Graphical Representations as Assessments of Engineering Thinking." In *Proceedings of the 117th American Society for Engineering Education Annual Conference & Exposition.* ASEE Conferences. https://doi.org/10.18260/1-2--16769.

Brydon-Miller, Mary, Davydd Greenwood, and Patricia Maguire. 2003. *Why Action Research? Action Research* 1 (1): 9–28. https://doi.org/10.1177/14767503030011002.

Caceffo, Ricardo, Steve Wolfman, Kellogg S. Booth, and Rodolfo Azevedo. 2016. "Developing a Computer Science Concept Inventory for Introductory Programming." In *SIGCSE '16: Proceedings of the 47th ACM Technical Symposium on Computing Science Education*, 364–69. Association for Computing Machinery. https://doi.org/10.1145/2839509.2844559.

Carlson, W. Bernard. 2003. "Toward a Philosophy of Engineering: The Fundamental Role of Representation." In *Proceedings of the 110th American Society for Engineering Education Annual Conference & Exposition.* ASEE Conferences. https://doi.org/10.18260/1-2--12063.

Chattopadhyay, Souti, Ishita Prasad, Austin Z. Henley, Anita Sarma, and Titus Barik. 2020. "What's Wrong With Computational Notebooks? Pain Points, Needs, and Design Opportunities." In *Proceedings of the 2020 CHI Conference on Human Factors in Computing Systems.* https://doi.org/10.1145/3313831.3376729.

Chi, Michelene T. H. 2011. "Theoretical Perspectives, Methodological Approaches, and Trends in the Study of Expertise." In *Expertise in Mathematics Instruction: An International Perspective.* Edited by Yeping Li and Gabriele Kaiser, 17–39. Boston: Springer.

Choi, Jeong-Im, and Michael Hannafin. 1995. "Situated Cognition and Learning Environments: Roles, Structures, and Implications for Design." *Educational Technology Research and Development* 43 (2): 53–69. https://doi.org/10.1007/BF02300472.

Collins, Allan, John Seely Brown, and Ann Holum. 1991. "Cognitive Apprenticeship: Making Thinking Visible." *American Educator* 15 (3): 6–11.

Collins, Allan, John Seely Brown, and Susan E. Newman. 1989. "Cognitive Apprenticeship: Teaching the Crafts of Reading, Writing, and Mathematics." In *Knowing, Learning, and Instruction: Essays in Honor of Robert Glaser.* Edited by Lauren B. Resnick, 32–42. Mahwah, NJ: Lawrence Erlbaum.

Collins, Allan, and Manu Kapur. 2014. "Cognitive Apprenticeship." In *The Cambridge Handbook of the Learning Sciences.* Edited by R. Keith Sawyer, 109–27. New York: Cambridge University Press.

CSTA (Computer Science Teachers Association). 2017. "CSTA K–12 Computer Science Standards, Revised 2017." https://csteachers.org/k12standards/.

Corcoran, Thomas B., Frederic A. Mosher, and Aaron Rogat. 2009. *Learning Progressions in Science: An Evidence-Based Approach to Reform.* CPRE Research Report # RR-63. Consortium for Policy Research in Education. https://www.cpre.org/sites/default/files/researchreport/829_lpsciencerr63.pdf.

CTGV (The Cognition Technology Group at Vanderbilt). 1990. "Anchored Instruction and Its Relationship to Situated Cognition." *Educational Researcher* 19 (6): 2–10. https://doi.org/10.3102/0013189X019006002.

Dane, Erik. 2010. "Reconsidering the Trade-Off Between Expertise and Flexibility: A Cognitive

Entrenchment Perspective." *Academy of Management Review* 35 (4): 579–603. https://doi.org/10 .5465/amr.35.4.zok579.

Davis, Rebekah, Kerri Brown Parker, and Laura Fogle. 2019. "A Case of Course Revision: Cognitive Apprenticeship and Critical Reflection for ICT in Teacher Preparation." In *Proceedings of Society for Information Technology & Teacher Education International Conference*, 1779–84. Association for the Advancement of Computing in Education (AACE).

Denning, Peter J. 2000. "Computer Science: The Discipline." In *Encyclopedia of Computer Science*. Edited by Anthony Ralston and David Hemmendinger. New York: Wiley.

Department for Education. 2013. *National Curriculum in England: Computing Programmes of Study*. https://www.gov.uk/government/publications/national-curriculum-in-england-computing -programmes-of-study.

Devens, P. E. 1999. "MATLAB & Freshman Engineering." In *Proceedings of the 1999 American Society for Engineering Education Annual Conference & Exposition*. ASEE Conferences. https:// peer.asee.org/7830.

Diefes-Dux, Heidi A., Margret A. Hjalmarson, and Judith S. Zawojewski. 2013. "Student Team Solutions to an Open-Ended Mathematical Modeling Problem: Gaining Insights for Educational Improvement." *Journal of Engineering Education* 102 (1): 179–216. https://doi.org/10 .1002/jee.20002.

Diefes-Dux, Heidi A., Tamara Moore, Judith Zawojewski, P. K. Imbrie, and Deborah Follman. 2004. "A Framework for Posing Open-Ended Engineering Problems: Model-Eliciting Activities." In *34th Annual Frontiers in Education, 2004. FIE 2004*. IEEE. https://doi.org/10.1109/FIE.2004 .1408556.

Diefes-Dux, Heidi A., Judith S. Zawojewski, Margret A. Hjalmarson, and Monica E. Cardella. 2012. "A Framework for Analyzing Feedback in a Formative Assessment System for Mathematical Modeling Problems." *Journal of Engineering Education* 101 (2): 375–406. https://doi.org/10.1002 /j.2168-9830.2012.tb00054.x.

DuBoulay, Benedict. 1986. "Some Difficulties of Learning to Program." In *Studying the Novice Programmer*. Edited by Elliot Soloway and James C. Spohrer. Mahwah, NJ: Lawrence Erlbaum.

Ertmer, Peggy A., and Timothy J. Newby. 1996. "The Expert Learner: Strategic, Self-Regulated, and Reflective." *Instructional Science* 24:1–24. https://doi.org/10.1007/BF00156001.

Feldon, David F., Kathan D. Shukla, and Michelle Anne Maher. 2016. "Faculty–Student Coauthorship as a Means to Enhance STEM Graduate Students' Research Skills." *International Journal for Researcher Development* 7 (2): 178–91. https://doi.org/10.1108/IJRD-10-2015-0027.

Fennell, Hayden W., Genisson Silva Coutinho, Alejandra J. Magana, David Restrepo, and Pablo D. Zavattieri. 2017. "Enhancing Student Meaning-Making of Threshold Concepts via Computation: The Case of Mohr's Circle." *Proceedings of the 2017 American Society for Engineering Education Annual Conference & Exposition*. ASEE Conferences. https://doi.org/10.18260/1-2--28279.

Fennell, Hayden W., Joseph A. Lyon, Aasakiran Madamanchi, and Alejandra J. Magana. 2020. "Toward Computational Apprenticeship: Bringing a Constructivist Agenda to Computational Pedagogy." *Journal of Engineering Education* 109 (2): 170–76. https://doi.org/10.1002/jee.20316.

Fennell, Hayden W., Joseph A. Lyon, Alejandra J. Magana, Sanjay Rebello, Carina M. Rebello, and Yuri B. Peidrahita. 2019. "Designing Hybrid Physics Labs: Combining Simulation and Experiment for Teaching Computational Thinking in First-Year Engineering." In *2019 IEEE*

Frontiers in Education Conference (FIE). https://doi.org/10.1109/FIE43999.2019.9028390.

Feurzeig, Wallace, and Nancy Roberts, eds. 1999. *Modeling and Simulation in Science and Mathematics Education*. New York: Springer.

Fila, Nicholas D., and Michael C. Loui. 2014. "Structured Pairing in a First-Year Electrical and Computer Engineering Laboratory: The Effects on Student Retention, Attitudes, and Teamwork." *International Journal of Engineering Education* 30 (4): 848–61.

Gannod, Gerald C., Janet E. Burge, and Michael T. Helmick. 2008. *Using the Inverted Classroom to Teach Software Engineering*. Technical report MU-SEAS-CSA-2007-001. Retrieved from Scholarly Commons at Miami University. https://sc.lib.miamioh.edu/bitstream/handle/2374.MIA/206/fulltext.pdf.

Gilmore, Joanna, Michelle Vieyra, Briana Timmerman, David Feldon, and Michelle Maher. 2015. "The Relationship Between Undergraduate Research Participation and Subsequent Research Performance of Early Career STEM Graduate Students." *Journal of Higher Education* 86 (6): 834–63. https://doi.org/10.1080/00221546.2015.11777386.

Gobert, Janice D., and Barbara C. Buckley. 2000. "Introduction to Model-Based Teaching and Learning in Science Education." *International Journal of Science Education* 22 (9): 891–94. https://doi.org/10.1080/095006900416839.

Goode, Joanna, and Jane Margolis. 2011. "Exploring Computer Science: A Case Study of School Reform." *ACM Transactions on Computing Education (TOCE)* 11 (2): 1–16. https://doi.org/10.1145/1993069.1993076.

Harrison, Allan G., and David F. Treagust. 2000. "A Typology of School Science Models." *International Journal of Science Education* 22 (9): 1011–26. https://doi.org/10.1080/095006900416884.

Hatano, Giyoo, and Kayoko Inagaki. 1986. "Two Courses of Expertise." In *Child Development and Education in Japan*. Edited by Harold Stevenson, Hiroshi Azuma, and Kenji Hakuta, 262–72. New York: W. H. Freeman.

Hatano, Giyoo, and Yoko Oura. 2003. "Commentary: Reconceptualizing School Learning Using Insight from Expertise Research." *Educational Researcher* 32 (8): 26–29. https://doi.org/10.3102/0013189X032008026.

Higley, Kelli, Thomas Litzinger, Peggy Van Meter, Christine B. Masters, and Jonna Kulikowich. 2007. "Effects of Conceptual Understanding, Math and Visualization Skills on Problem-Solving in Statics." In *Proceedings of the 114th American Society for Engineering Education Annual Conference & Exposition*. ASEE Conferences. https://doi.org/10.18260/1-2--2382.

Hrynuk, John, Matthew Pennington, David Illig, and John P. Dempsey. 2008. "Freshman Engineering: An Introductory Computer Course Teaching MATLAB and LABVIEW." In *Proceedings of the 2008 American Society for Engineering Education Annual Conference & Exposition*. ASEE Conferences. https://doi.org/10.18260/1-2--3841.

Hu, Chenglie. 2007. "Integrating Modern Research Into Numerical Computation Education." *Computing in Science & Engineering* 9 (5): 78–81. https://doi.org/10.1109/MCSE.2007.100.

Jaiswal, Aparajita, Joseph A. Lyon, Yiqun Zhang, and Alejandra J. Magana. 2021. "Supporting Student Reflective Practices Through Modelling-Based Learning Assignments." *European Journal of Engineering Education* 46 (6): 987–1006. https://doi.org/10.1080/03043797.2021.1952164.

Johnson-Laird, Philip N. 1995. "Mental Models, Deductive Reasoning, and the Brain." *The Cognitive Neurosciences* 65:999–1008.

Jonassen, David, Johannes Strobel, and Chwee Beng Lee. 2006. "Everyday Problem Solving in

Engineering: Lessons for Engineering Educators." *Journal of Engineering Education* 95 (2): 139–51. https://doi.org/10.1002/j.2168-9830.2006.tb00885.x.

Kafai, Yasmin, Kristin Searle, Cîstobal Martinez, and Bryan Brayboy. 2014. "Ethnocomputing With Electronic Textiles: Culturally Responsive Open Design to Broaden Participation in Computing in American Indian Youth and Communities." In *SIGCSE '14: Proceedings of the 45th ACM Technical Symposium on Computer Science Education*, 241–46. Association for Computing Machinery. https://doi.org/10.1145/2538862.2538903.

Kapur, Manu. 2010. "Productive Failure in Mathematical Problem Solving." *Instructional Science* 38 (6): 523–50. https://doi.org/10.1007/s11251-009-9093-x.

Kapur, Manu, and Katerine Bielaczyc. 2012. "Designing for Productive Failure." *Journal of the Learning Sciences* 21 (1): 45–83. https://doi.org/10.1080/10508406.2011.591717.

Klever, Nik. 2020. "Jupyter Notebook, JupyterHub and Nbgrader." In *Becoming Greener—Digitalization in My Work*. Edited by T. Mirola, 37–43. Lappeenranta, Finland: LAB University of Applied Sciences.

Kolb, David A., Richard E. Boyatzis, and Charalampos Mainemelis. 2011. "Experiential Learning Theory: Previous Research and New Directions." In *Perspectives on Thinking, Learning, and Cognitive Styles*. Edited by Robert J. Sternberg, Li-fang Zhang, 227–48. New York: Routledge.

Lage, Maureen J., Glenn J. Platt, and Michael Treglia. 2000. "Inverting the Classroom: A Gateway to Creating an Inclusive Learning Environment." *Journal of Economic Education* 31 (1): 30–43. https://doi.org/10.1080/00220480009596759.

Landau, Rubin. 2006. "Computational Physics: A Better Model for Physics Education?" *Computing in Science & Engineering* 8 (5): 22–30. https://doi.org/10.1109/MCSE.2006.85.

Lave, Jean, and Wenger, Etienne. 1991. *Situated Learning: Legitimate Peripheral Participation*. Cambridge University Press.

Lee, Irene, Fred Martin, Jill Denner, Bob Coulter, Walter Allan, Jeri Erickson, Joyce Malyn-Smith, and Linda Werner. 2011. "Computational Thinking for Youth in Practice." *ACM Inroads* 2 (1): 32–37. https://users.soe.ucsc.edu/~linda/pubs/ACMInroads.pdf.

Lehrer, Richard, and Leona Schauble. 2000. "Developing Model-Based Reasoning in Mathematics and Science." *Journal of Applied Developmental Psychology* 21 (1): 39–48. https://doi.org/10.1016/S0193-3973(99)00049-0.

Lesh, Richard, Mark Hoover, Bonnie Hole, Anthony Kelly, and Thomas Post. 2011. "Principles for Developing Thought-Revealing Activities for Students and Teachers." In *Handbook of Research Design in Mathematics and Science Education*. Edited by Anthony E. Kelly and Richard A. Lesh, 591–645. New York: Routledge.

Lister, Raymond, Elizabeth S. Adams, Sue Fitzgerald, William Fone, John Hamer, Morten Lindholm, Robert McCartney, Jan Erik Moström, Kate Sanders, Otto Seppälä, Beth Simon, and Lynda Thomas. 2004. "A Multi-National Study of Reading and Tracing Skills in Novice Programmers." *ACM SIGCSE Bulletin* 36 (4): 119–50. https://doi.org/10.1145/1041624.1041673.

Löhner, Simone, Wouter R. van Joolingen, Elwin R. Savelsbergh, and Bernadette van Hout-Wolters. 2005. "Students' Reasoning during Modeling in an Inquiry Learning Environment." *Computers in Human Behavior* 21 (3): 441–61. https://doi.org/10.1016/j.chb.2004.10.037.

Louca, Loucas T., and Zacharias C. Zacharia. 2012. "Modeling-Based Learning in Science Education: Cognitive, Metacognitive, Social, Material and Epistemological Contributions." *Educational Review* 64 (4): 471–92. https://doi.org/10.1080/00131911.2011.628748.

Lucas Lacal, Miguel. 2020. "Platform for Automatically Generating and Correcting Python Programming Exercises." BS thesis, informatics engineering, industrial, informatics, and telecommunication engineering, Universidad Publica de Navarra. https://academica-e.unavarra.es/xmlui/handle/2454/37600.

Luchini, K., D. Colbry, and W. Punch. 2007. "Designing Introductory Programming Courses for Graduate and Undergraduate Students: A Parallel Case Study." In *Proceedings of the 2007 American Society for Engineering Education Annual Conference & Exposition*. ASEE Conferences.

Lyon, Joseph A., Aparajita Jaiswal, and Alejandra J. Magana. 2020. "The Use of MATLAB Live as a Technology-Enabled Learning Environment for Computational Modeling Activities Within a Capstone Engineering Course." In Proceedings of the *127th Annual American Society for Engineering Education Annual Conference & Exposition*. ASEE Conferences. https://doi.org/10.18260/1-2--35380.

Lyon, Joseph A., and Alejandra J. Magana. 2020. "Computational Thinking in Higher Education: A Review of the Literature." *Computer Applications in Engineering Education* 28 (5): 1174–89. https://doi.org/10.1002/cae.22295.

Lyon, Joseph A., and Alejandra J. Magana. 2021. "The Use of Engineering Model-Building Activities to Elicit Computational Thinking: A Design-Based Research Study." *Journal of Engineering Education* 110 (1): 184–206. https://doi.org/10.1002/jee.20372.

Lyon, Joseph A., Alejandra J. Magana, and Martin R. Okos. 2019. "Work in Progress: Designing Modeling-Based Learning Environments Within a Capstone Engineering Course." In *Proceedings of the 126th Annual American Society for Engineering Education Annual Conference & Exposition*. ASEE Conferences. https://doi.org 10.18260/1-2--33604/.

Lyon, Joseph A., Alejandra J. Magana, and Ruth A. Streveler. 2022. "Characterizing Computational Thinking in the Context of Model-Planning Activities." *Modelling* 3 (3): 344–58. https://doi.org/10.3390/modelling3030022.

Lyons, Kayley, Jacqueline E. McLaughlin, Julia Khanova, and Mary T. Roth. 2017. "Cognitive Apprenticeship in Health Sciences Education: A Qualitative Review." *Advances in Health Sciences Education* 22 (2017): 723–39. https://doi.org/10.1007/s10459-016-9707-4.

Lytle, Nicholas, Veronica Cateté, Danielle Boulden, Yihuan Dong, Jennifer Houchins, Alexandra Milliken, Amy Isvik, Dolly Bounajim, Eric Wiebe, and Tiffany Barnes. 2019. "Use, Modify, Create: Comparing Computational Thinking Lesson Progressions for Stem Classes." In *ITiCSE '19: Proceedings of the 2019 ACM Conference on Innovation and Technology in Computer Science Education*, 395–401. https://doi.org/10.1145/3304221.3319786.

Mackillop, Lucy, Jo Parker-Swift, and Jim Crossley. 2011. "Getting the Questions Right: Noncompound Questions Are More Reliable Than Compound Questions on Matched Multi-source Feedback Instruments." *Medical Education* 45 (8): 843–48. https://doi.org/10.1111/j.1365-2923.2011.03996.x.

Magana, Alejandra J. 2017. "Modeling and Simulation in Engineering Education: A Learning Progression." *Journal of Professional Issues in Engineering Education and Practice* 143 (4): 1–19. https://doi.org/10.1061/(ASCE)EI.1943-5541.0000338.

Magana, Alejandra J. 2022. "The Role of Frameworks in Engineering Education Research." *Journal of Engineering Education* 111 (1): 9–13. https://doi.org/10.1002/jee.20443.

Magana, Alejandra J., Sean P. Brophy, and George M. Bodner. 2012. "Student Views of Engineering Professors Technological Pedagogical Content Knowledge for Integrating Computational

Simulation Tools in Nanoscale Science and Engineering." *International Journal of Engineering Education* 28 (5): 1033–45.

Magana, Alejandra J., and Genisson Silva Coutinho. 2017. "Modeling and Simulation Practices for a Computational Thinking-Enabled Engineering Workforce." *Computer Applications in Engineering Education* 25 (1): 62–78. https://doi.org/10.1002/cae.21779.

Magana, Alejandra J., Michael L. Falk, and Michael J. Reese. 2013. "Introducing Discipline-Based Computing in Undergraduate Engineering Education." *ACM Transactions on Computing Education* 13 (4): 1–22. https://doi.org/10.1145/2534971.

Magana, Alejandra J., Michael L. Falk, Camilo Vieira, and Michael J. Reese Jr. 2016. "A Case Study of Undergraduate Engineering Students' Computational Literacy and Self-Beliefs About Computing in the Context of Authentic Practices." *Computers in Human Behavior* 61:427–42. https://doi.org/10.1016/j.chb.2016.03.025.

Magana, Alejandra J., Michael L. Falk, Camilo Vieira, Micharl J. Reese Jr., Oluwatosin Alabi, and Sylvain Patinet. 2017. "Affordances and Challenges of Computational Tools for Supporting Modeling and Simulation Practices." *Computer Applications in Engineering Education* 25 (3): 352–75. https://doi.org/10.1002/cae.21804.

Magana, Alejandra J., Hayden W. Fennell, Camilo Vieira, and Michael L. Falk. 2019. "Characterizing the Interplay of Cognitive and Metacognitive Knowledge in Computational Modeling and Simulation Practices." *Journal of Engineering Education* 108 (2): 276–303. https://doi.org/10.1002/jee.20264.

Magana, Alejandra J., Juan D. Ortega-Alvarez, Ryan Lovan, Daniel Gómez Pizano, Johannio Marulanda, and Shirley Dyke. 2017. "Virtual, Local and Remote Laboratories for Conceptual Understanding of Dynamic Systems." *International Journal of Engineering Education* 33 (1): 91–105.

Magana, Alejandra J., Camilo Vieira, Hayden W. Fennell, Anindya Roy, and Michael L. Falk. 2020. "Undergraduate Engineering Students' Types and Quality of Knowledge Used in Synthetic Modeling." *Cognition and Instruction.* 38 (4): 503–37. https://doi.org/10.1080/07370008.2020.1792912.

Malyn-Smith, Joyce, and Irene Lee. 2012. "Application of the Occupational Analysis of Computational Thinking-Enabled STEM Professionals as a Program Assessment Tool." *Journal of Computational Science Education* 3 (1): 2–10. https://doi.org/10.22369/issn.2153-4136/3/1/1.

Maria, Anu. 1997. "Introduction to Modeling and Simulation." In *WSC '97: Proceedings of the 29th Conference on Winter Simulation.* https://doi.org/10.1145/268437.268440.

McCracken, Michael, Vicki Almstrum, Danny Diaz, Mark Guzdial, Dianne Hagan, Yifat Ben-David Kolikant, Cary Laxer, Lynda Thomas, Ian Utting, and Tadeusz Wilusz. 2001. "A Multinational, Multi-institutional Study of Assessment of Programming Skills of First-Year CS Students." *ACM SIGCSE Bulletin* 33 (4): 125–80. https://doi.org/10.1145/572133.572137.

McNeill, Katherine L., and Joseph Krajcik. 2008. "Inquiry and Scientific Explanations: Helping Students Use Evidence and Reasoning." In *Science as Inquiry in the Secondary Setting.* Edited by Julie Luft, Randy L. Bell, and Julie Gess-Newsome, 121–34. Arlington, VA: National Science Teachers Association.

Merritt, Chris, Michelle Daniel, Brendan W. Munzer, Mariann Nocera, Joshua C. Ross, and Sally A. Santen. 2018. "A Cognitive Apprenticeship-Based Faculty Development Intervention for Emergency Medicine Educators." *Western Journal of Emergency Medicine* 19 (1): 198–204. https://doi.org/10.5811/westjem.2017.11.36429.

Morrell, Darryl. 2007. "Design of an Introductory MATLAB Course for Freshman Engineering Students." In *Proceedings of the 2007 American Society for Engineering Education Annual Conference & Exposition*. ASEE Conferences. https://doi.org/10.18260/1-2--1654.

Morris, Phillip J., Lyle N. Long, and Ali Haghighat, and Martin L. Brady. 1996. "Curriculum Development in Advanced Computation." In *Proceedings of the 1996 American Society for Engineering Education Annual Conference & Exposition*. ASEE Conferences. https://doi.org/10.18260/1-2--5954.

Mselle, Leonard J., and Hashim Twaakyondo. 2012. "The Impact of Memory Transfer Language (MTL) on Reducing Misconceptions in Teaching Programming to Novices." *International Journal of Machine Learning and Applications* 1 (1): 6.

Narayanan, Ganapathy. 2007. "Teaching of Essential MATLAB Commands in Applied Mathematics Course for Engineering Technology." In *Proceedings of the 2007 American Society for Engineering Education Annual Conference & Exposition*. ASEE Conferences. https://doi.org/10.18260/1-2--3052.

NASEM (National Academies of Sciences, Engineering, and Medicine). 2018. *Data Science for Undergraduates: Opportunities and Options*. Washington, DC: The National Academies Press.

Nersessian, Nancy J. 1999. "Model-Based Reasoning in Conceptual Change." In *Model-Based Reasoning in Scientific Discovery*. Edited by Lorenzo Magnani, Nancy J. Nersessian and Paul Thagard, 5–57. New York: Kluwer Academic/Plenum Publishers.

Nersessian, Nancy J. 2002. "The Cognitive Basis of Model-Based Reasoning in Science." In *The Cognitive Basis of Science*. Edited by Peter Carruthers, Stephen Stich, and Michael Siegal, 133–53. Cambridge: Cambridge University Press.

Noroozi, Omid, Paul A. Kirschner, Harm J. A. Biemans, and Martin Mulder. 2018. "Promoting Argumentation Competence: Extending from First-To Second-Order Scaffolding Through Adaptive Fading." *Educational Psychology Review* 30 (1): 153–76. https://doi.org/10.1007/s10648-017-9400-z.

NRC (National Research Council). 2011. *Report of a Workshop on the Pedagogical Aspects of Computational Thinking*. Washington, DC: National Research Council of the National Academies.

NRC (National Research Council). 2012. *Discipline-Based Education Research. Understanding and Improving Learning in Undergraduate Science and Engineering*. Washington, DC: National Research Council of the National Academies.

O'Hara, Keith J., Doug Blank, and James Marshall. 2015. "Computational Notebooks for AI Education." In *Proceedings of the Twenty-Eighth International Florida Artificial Intelligence Research Society Conference*. Association for the Advancement of Artificial Intelligence. https://repository.brynmawr.edu/cgi/viewcontent.cgi?article=1030&context=compsci_pubs.

Ortega-Alvarez, Juan D., William Sanchez, and Alejandra J. Magana. 2018. "Exploring Undergraduate Students' Computational Modeling Abilities and Conceptual Understanding of Electric Circuits." *IEEE Transactions on Education* 66 (3): 204–13. https://doi.org/0.1109/TE.2018.2822245.

Ottesen, Johnny T., Mette S. Olufsen, and Jesper K. Larsen. 2006. *Applied Mathematical Models in Human Physiology*. Roskilde, Denmark: Roskilde University.

Pea, Roy D., and D. Midian Kurland. 1983. *On the Cognitive Prerequisites of Learning Computer Programming*. Technical Report No. 18. Washington, DC: National Institute of Education. https://eric.ed.gov/?id=ED249931.

Pellegrino, James W., Naomi Chudowsky, and Robert Glaser. 2001. *Knowing What Students Know: The Science and Design of Educational Assessment.* Washington, DC: National Academy Press.

Peters-Burton, Erin E., Sydney A. Merz, Erin M. Ramirez, and Maryam Saroughi. 2015. "The Effect of Cognitive Apprenticeship-Based Professional Development on Teacher Self-Efficacy of Science Teaching, Motivation, Knowledge Calibration, and Perceptions of Inquiry-Based Teaching." *Journal of Science Teacher Education* 26:525–48. https://doi.org/10.1007/s10972-015-9436-1.

Quintana, Chris, Brian J. Reiser, Elizabeth A. Davis, Joseph Krajcik, Eric Fretz, Ravit Golan Duncan, Eleni Kyza, Daniel Edelson, and Elliot Soloway. 2004. "A Scaffolding Design Framework for Software to Support Science Inquiry." *Journal of the Learning Sciences* 13 (3): 337–86. https://doi.org/10.1207/s15327809jls1303_4.

Riel, M. 2023. "Understanding Action Research." Center for Collaborative Action Research. Accessed October 2023. https://www.ccarweb.org/what-is-action-research.

Sadler, Troy D., Stephen Burgin, Lyle McKinney, and Luis Ponjuan. 2010. "Learning Science Through Research Apprenticeships: A Critical Review of the Literature." *Journal of Research in Science Teaching* 47 (3): 235–56. https://doi.org/10.1002/tea.20326.

Sanchez-Peña, Matilde, Camilo Vieira, and Alejandra J. Magana. 2022. "Data Science Knowledge Integration: Affordances of a Computational Cognitive Apprenticeship on Student Conceptual Understanding." *Computer Applications in Engineering Education.* https://doi.org/10.1002/cae.22580.

Schwartz, Daniel L., John D. Bransford, and David Sears. 2005. "Efficiency and Innovation in Transfer." In *Transfer of Learning from a Modern Multidisciplinary Perspective.* Edited by Jose P. Mestre, 1–51. Greenwich, CT: Information Age Publishing.

Schwartz, Daniel L., Catherine C. Chase, Marily A. Oppezzo, and Doris B. Chin. 2011. "Practicing versus Inventing With Contrasting Cases: The Effects of Telling First on Learning and Transfer." *Journal of Educational Psychology* 103 (4): 759–75. https://doi.org/10.1037/a0025140.

Schwarz, Christina V., Brian J. Reiser, Elizabeth A. Davis, Lisa Kenyon, Andres Achér, David Fortus, Yael Shwartz, Barbara Hug, and Joe Krajcik. 2009. "Developing a Learning Progression for Scientific Modeling: Making Scientific Modeling Accessible and Meaningful for Learners." *Journal of Research in Science Teaching* 46 (6): 632–54. https://doi.org/10.1002/tea.20311.

Shaikh, Uzma, Alejandra J. Magana, Camilo Vieira, and R. Edwin Garcia. 2015. "An Exploratory Study of the Role of Modeling and Simulation in Supporting or Hindering Engineering Students' Problem-Solving Skills." In *Proceedings of the 2015 American Society for Engineering Education Annual Conference & Exposition.* ASEE Conferences. https://doi.org/10.18260/p.23524.

Shiflet, Angela B., and George W. Shiflet. 2014. *Introduction to Computational Science: Modeling and Simulation for the Sciences.* Princeton, NJ: Princeton University Press.

Sigel, Irving E. 1999. *Development of Mental Representation: Theories and Applications.* Mahwah, NJ: Lawrence Erlbaum.

Soloway, Elliot, and James C. Spohrer, eds. 1989. *Studying the Novice Programmer.* Mahwah, NJ: Lawrence Erlbaum.

Stickel, Micah. 2011. "Putting Mathematics in Context: An Integrative Approach Using MATLAB." In *Proceedings of the 2011 American Society for Engineering Education Annual Conference & Exposition.* ASEE Conferences. https://doi.org/10.18260/1-2--18843.

Sticklen, Jon, Marilyn Amey, Taner Eskil, Timothy Hinds, and Mark Urban-Lurain. 2004. "Application of Object-Centered Scaffolding to Introductory MATLAB." In *Proceedings of the 2004 American Society for Engineering Education Annual Conference & Exposition*. ASEE Conferences. https://doi.org/10.18260/1-2--13123.

Sweller, John, Jeroen J. G. van Merriënboer, and Fred Paas. 2019. "Cognitive Architecture and Instructional Design: 20 Years Later." *Educational Psychology Review* 31 (2): 261–92. https://doi.org/10.1007/s10648-019-09465-5.

Tang, Xiaodan, Yue Yin, Qiao Lin, Roxana Hadad, and Xiaoming Zhai. 2020. "Assessing Computational Thinking: A Systematic Review of Empirical Studies." *Computers & Education* 148 (April): 103798. https://doi.org/10.1016/j.compedu.2019.103798.

Tew, Allison Elliott, and Mark Guzdial. 2010. "Developing a Validated Assessment of Fundamental CS1 Concepts." In *SIGCSE '10: Proceedings of the 41st ACM Technical Symposium on Computer Science Education*. Association for Computing Machinery. https://doi.org/10.1145/1734263.1734297.

Traxler, Adrienne, Rachel Henderson, John Stewart, Gay Stewart, Alexis Papak, and Rebecca Lindell. 2018. "Gender Fairness Within the Force Concept Inventory." *Physical Review Physics Education Research* 14 (1): 010103. https://doi.org/10.1103/PhysRevPhysEducRes.14.010103.

VanLehn, Kurt. 2013. "Model Construction as a Learning Activity: A Design Space and Review." *Interactive Learning Environments* 21 (4): 371–13. https://doi.org/10.1080/10494820.2013.803125.

Vieira, Camilo, Ricardo L. Gómez, Margarita Gómez, Michael Canu, and Mauricio Duque. 2023. "Implementing Unplugged CS and Use-Modify-Create to Develop Student Computational Thinking Skills." *Educational Technology & Society* 26 (3): 155–75. https://www.jstor.org/stable/48734328.

Vieira, Camilo, Alejandra J. Magana, Michael L. Falk, and R. Edwin García. 2017. "Writing In-Code Comments to Self-Explain in Computational Science and Engineering Education." *ACM Transactions on Computing Education (TOCE)* 17 (4): 17:01–17:21. https://doi.org/10.1145/3058751.

Vieira, Camilo, Alejandra J. Magana, R. Edwin García, Aniruddha Jana, and Matthew Krafcik. 2018. "Integrating Computational Science Tools into a Thermodynamics Course." *Journal of Science Education and Technology* 27 (1): 1–12. https://doi.org/10.1007/s10956-017-9726-9.

Vieira, Camilo, Alejandra J. Magana, Anindya Roy, and Michael L. Falk. 2019. "Student Explanations in the Context of Computational Science and Engineering Education." *Cognition and Instruction* 32 (7): 201–31. https://doi.org/10.1080/07370008.2018.1539738.

Vieira, Camilo, Alejandra J. Magana, Anindya Roy, and Michael Falk. 2020. "Providing Students With Agency to Self-Scaffold in a Computational Science and Engineering Course." *Journal of Computing in Higher Education* 33:328–66. https://doi.org/10.1007/s12528-020-09267-7.

Vieira, Camilo, Alejandra J. Magana, Anindya Roy, Michael L. Falk, and Michael J. Reese Jr. 2015. "Exploring Undergraduate Students' Computational Literacy in the Context of Problem Solving." In *Proceedings of the 122nd American Society for Engineering Education Annual Conference & Exposition* ASEE Conferences. https://doi.org/10.18260/p.24081.

Vieira, Camilo, Alejandra J. Magana, Anindya Roy, Michael L. Falk, and Michael J. Reese Jr. 2016. "Exploring Undergraduate Students' Computational Literacy in the Context of Problem Solving." *Computers in Education Journal* 7 (1): 100–12. https://coed.asee.org/wp-content/uploads/2020/08/11-Exploring-Undergraduate-Students-Computational-Literacy-in-the-Context-of-Problem-Solving.pdf.

Vieira, Camilo, Anindya Roy, Alejandra J. Magana, Michael L. Falk, and Michael J. Reese Jr. 2016. "In-Code Comments as a Self-Explanation Strategy for Computational Science Education." In

Proceedings of the 123rd American Society for Engineering Education Annual Conference & Exposition. ASEE Conferences. https://doi.org/10.18260/p.25642.

Vieira, Camilo, Junchao Yan, and Alejandra J. Magana. 2015. "Exploring Design Characteristics of Worked Examples to Support Programming and Algorithm Design." *Journal of Computational Science Education* 6 (1): 2–15. https://doi.org/10.22369/issn.2153-4136/6/1/1.

Vihavainen, Arto, Matti Paksula, and Matti Luukkainen. 2011. "Extreme Apprenticeship Method in Teaching Programming for Beginners." In *SIGCSE '11: Proceedings of the 42nd ACM Technical Symposium on Computer Science Education*, 93–98. Association for Computing Machinery. https://doi.org/10.1145/1953163.1953196.

Wang, April Yi, Anant Mittal, Christopher Brooks, and Steve Oney. 2019. "How Data Scientists Use Computational Notebooks for Real-Time Collaboration." In *Proceedings of the ACM on Human-Computer Interaction* 3 (CSCW): 9:1–9:30. https://doi.org/10.1145/3359141.

Weintrop, David, Elham Beheshti, Michael Horn, Kai Orton, Kemi Jona, Laura Trouille, and Uri Wilensky. 2016. "Defining Computational Thinking for Mathematics and Science Classrooms." *Journal of Science Education and Technology* 25 (1): 127–47. https://doi.org/10.1007/s10956-015-9581-5.

Wiggins, Grant, and Jay McTighe. 1997. *Understanding by Design.* Alexandria, VA: Association for Supervision and Curriculum Development.

Wiggins, Grant, and Jay McTighe. 2005. *Understanding by Design.* Expanded 2nd ed. San Francisco: Pearson Education.

Yadav, Aman, Chris Stephenson, and Hai Hong. 2017. "Computational Thinking for Teacher Education." *Communications of the ACM* 60 (4): 55–62. https://doi.org/10.1145/2994591.

Yardi, Sarita, and Amy Bruckman. 2007. "What Is Computing? Bridging the Gap Between Teenagers' Perceptions and Graduate Students' Experiences." In *ICER '07: Proceedings of the Third International Workshop on Computing Education Research*, 39–50. Association for Computing Machinery.

Yasar, Osman, Kulathur S. Rajasethupathy, Robert E. Tuzun, R. Alan McCoy, and Joseph Harkin. 2000. "A New Perspective Computational Science Education." *Computational Science Engineering* 5 (September/October): 74–79.

INDEX

Page numbers in italics indicate figures and tables

ABOUT THE CONTRIBUTORS

Michael L. Falk is a professor of materials science and engineering, mechanical engineering, and physics at Johns Hopkins University, where he currently serves as the vice dean for undergraduate education in the Whiting School of Engineering. Professor Falk earned a bachelor's degree in physics and a master's degree in computer science from Johns Hopkins University and a PhD in physics from the University of California, Santa Barbara. His research focuses on utilizing computer simulation at the atomic scale to understand what happens when materials are pushed out of equilibrium by processes such as bending, breaking, charging, and undergoing frictional sliding. He has also undertaken educational research on how engineering students best learn computing and two National Science Foundation–funded partnerships with the Baltimore City Schools to increase the engagement of students, teachers, and communities in STEM learning. Professor Falk has also been a strong advocate for diversity, particularly in creating a welcoming climate for LGBTQ people within the engineering and physics professions. He is a fellow of the American Physical Society and a recipient of the Materials Research Society Impact Award.

Hayden W. Fennell, MSE, is a researcher in the Department of Intelligent Systems Engineering at Indiana University Bloomington. He holds a BS in mechanical engineering from the University of South Carolina and an MSE in materials science and engineering from Johns Hopkins University. His current work focuses on the development of effective instructional tools for teaching computational modeling of virtual tissues and other biological systems to learners from a broad range of backgrounds. His research interests include characterizing and optimizing the development of transferrable computational expertise during the undergraduate engineering curriculum, as well as the design of pedagogical structures for teaching discipline-situated computational modeling skills in a variety of STEM settings.

Joseph A. Lyon, PhD, is a continuing lecturer for the College of Engineering at Purdue University in West Lafayette, Indiana. He holds a BS in bioengineering and an MS in industrial engineering, both from Purdue and earned his PhD in engineering education at Purdue, studying how engineering students best learn to program in classroom environments. Dr. Lyon is a 2018 recipient of the National Science Foundation's Graduate Research Fellowship. He spent multiple years working as an engineer in the food industry. His research interests focus on how computer programming is best learned in the engineering classroom and how to create computational pedagogy that broadens participation, increases engagement, and ensures retention across the undergraduate curriculum.

Camilo Vieira, PhD, is an assistant professor in the Department of Education at Universidad del Norte (UniNorte, Barranquilla, Colombia). He holds a BSc in systems engineering and a master's degree in engineering from Universidad Eafit (Colombia) and a PhD in technology (major concentration in computational sciences and engineering) from Purdue University. Dr. Vieira completed a postdoctoral experience at Purdue in information visualization and has been working at UniNorte since 2019, where he coordinates the research group Informática Educativa. In 2022, he was a Fulbright Visiting Scholar in the Department of Curriculum, Instruction, and Special Education at the University of Virginia. He investigates how to support student complex learning and how instructors teach complex topics, particularly in computing and engineering education. He also explores how to use computational methods to understand educational phenomena.

ABOUT THE AUTHOR

ALEJANDRA J. MAGANA, PHD, IS THE W.C. FURNAS PROFESSOR IN ENTERPRISE EX- cellence in the Department of Computer and Information Technology and professor in the School of Engineering Education at Purdue University. Dr. Magana holds a BE in information systems and an MS in technology, both from Tec de Monterrey, and an MS in educational technology and a PhD in engineering education, both from Purdue University. Her research program investigates how model-based cognition in science, technology, engineering, and mathematics (STEM) can be better supported by computational disciplinary practices such as computation, modeling and simulation, data science practices, and artificial intelligence. Currently Dr. Magana serves as deputy editor for the *Journal of Engineering Education*, co-editor of the Education Department for *IEEE Computer Graphics & Applications*, and associate editor for *Computer Applications in Engineering Education*.

As of 2023, Dr. Magana has published 92 refereed journal articles along with 105 peer-reviewed conference proceedings. Her work has been cited over 2,500 times since 2012 with an h-index of 28, and she has performed over 160 manuscript reviews. In 2015, Dr. Magana received the Faculty Early Career Development (CAREER) Award, the National Science Foundation's most prestigious award for faculty who exemplify the role of teacher-scholar through outstanding research, excellent education, and their integration within the context of the mission of their organization. In addition, she has secured over $23 million in federal funding from the National Science Foundation serving as principal or co-principal investigator.

Dr. Magana has been honored at the national level with three early career faculty awards: in 2010 from the American Educational Research Association, in 2012 from the American Society of Engineering Education, and in 2014 from the International Society of the Learning Sciences. In 2016, she was conferred the status of Purdue Faculty Scholar for being on an accelerated path toward academic distinction. In 2022, she was inducted into the Purdue University Teaching Academy, recognizing her excellence in teaching.